Business Benefits through Programme and Project Management

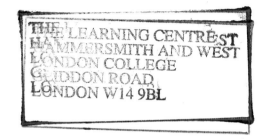

Office of Government Commerce

London: TSO

Published by TSO (The Stationery Office) and available from:

Online
www.tsoshop.co.uk

Mail, Telephone, Fax & E-mail
TSO
PO Box 29, Norwich, NR3 1GN
Telephone orders/General enquiries: 0870 600 5522
Fax orders: 0870 600 5533
E-mail: customer.services@tso.co.uk
Textphone: 0870 240 3701

TSO Shops
123 Kingsway, London, WC2B 6PQ
020 7242 6393 Fax 020 7242 6394
16 Arthur Street, Belfast BT1 4GD
028 9023 8451 Fax 028 9023 5401
71 Lothian Road, Edinburgh EH3 9AZ
0870 606 5566 Fax 0870 606 5588

TSO@Blackwell and other Accredited Agents

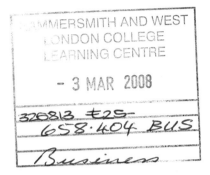
Published for the Office of Government Commerce under licence from the Controller of Her Majesty's Stationery Office.

First published 2006
Second impression 2006

ISBN-10 0 11 331025 0
ISBN-13 978 0 11 331025 8

Printed in the United Kingdom for The Stationery Office

N5449914 C20 10/06

CONTENTS

ACKNOWLEDGEMENTS

The Stationery Office, on behalf of OGC, acknowledges with thanks the contribution of David Greenly of Red Door Consulting to the first edition of this publication and that of Graham Williams of GSW Consultancy Limited for the material added to this second edition.

In addition TSO and OGC would like to recognise the input of the following individuals, who acted as reviewers:

Sandra Lomax (Audit Commission)
Neal Barcoe (user)
Alan Ferguson (AFA Project Management)
Rubina Faber (Regal Training Ltd)
Nick Tyler (user)
Ian Santry (user)
Tim Reeks (HM Revenue & Customs)

1
INTRODUCTION

Senior management is responsible for two key aspects of its business:

- Managing today's business operations. This involves maintaining business as usual in order to serve its customer base

- Shaping the organisation's longer-term strategies. This involves looking forward and deciding how the business needs to change to continue to serve its existing customer base or new customer bases in the future. The result should be new or transformed business operations.

This book addresses the second of these responsibilities with its focus on the need for successful organisations to be able to embrace change. Change can appear in many forms. One useful distinction is the difference between 'bounded' and 'unbounded' changes.

Bounded changes are where the scope of the change is strictly limited; the objectives of the change effort are clear and well understood; the nature of the problem is clear and so is what needs to change; relevant solutions are easily identified; and the change can be considered largely in isolation from its environment.

Unbounded changes, on the other hand, are where the scope is essentially unbounded; the objectives of the change effort are unclear and there is little agreement on objectives amongst parties involved; the nature of the problem is not clear; indeed, there may be disagreement over what the problem is and what needs to be changed; it is unclear what would constitute a solution; and the change must be considered in the context of its environment.

Traditionally, any changes required to deliver the new strategies of the organisation would have been implemented through projects. However, whilst projects are effective for the delivery of predefined products or outputs (bounded changes), they have not always proved successful in achieving the outcomes required of large-scale fundamental (unbounded) change. Where there is a major change there will be complexity and risk, and there are usually many interdependencies to manage between multiple projects and operations and there will be conflicting priorities to resolve. In these circumstances, programme management provides a more effective framework to help organisations deliver the required change.

Whether organisations are implementing bounded or unbounded change, experience shows that using formal approaches to programme and project management is the most effective way to deliver change well. This book presents the arguments to support that assertion. It describes and recommends the adoption of *Managing Successful Programmes* (MSP) and *Managing Successful Projects with PRINCE2* (PRINCE2) to provide an organisation with a fast track to successful programme and project management and the business benefits that will follow. These proven programme and project management approaches, MSP and PRINCE2, are described in terms of their generic features with a focus on the benefits these provide to the senior management team.

Programmes and their attendant projects are the key enablers for transforming business aspirations (business strategy) into manageable actions (changes), which deliver tangible business results (benefits). Although an organisation will take benefit from improving the level of control surrounding change, the step-change in performance will only follow where the disciplines of a combined Programme and Project Management Environment are integrated into the strategic planning and delivery processes too. Understanding the organisation's programme and project capability provides senior management with an invaluable tool for testing the feasibility of the strategy: there is little value in developing ambitious plans if there is not a delivery mechanism available to achieve them. For many organisations the realisation of business benefits from programme and project management will require a significant cultural shift from the random 'hit and miss' approach to one that demands more control and discipline, from the top of the organisation to the operational level.

To succeed, the cultural transition must be rooted in the very heart of the business and programme and project management nurtured to grow into a core capability of the organisation. This will only happen if there is ownership and determined leadership from the most senior managers. The upside of this for senior management is that MSP and PRINCE2 provide frameworks within which they can confidently delegate the planning and execution of change with a greatly increased probability of success by ensuring

- Clarity of purpose, where the justification and objectives of programmes and projects are clearly understood by mapping them against the big picture of where the organisation is going
- Credible planning, where the implementation of strategy is tested by looking at the programme and project capability and the capacity available to manage the changes required
- Commitment, where buy-in is achieved from all areas of the organisation through effective communication processes
- Control, where programmes and projects are planned and delivered in phases allowing for important review points.

Window on practice 1.1 summarises the experiences of an organisation that transformed itself from an 'also-ran' to the leader in its industry. Key to this was the early recognition that a revolution in working practices for the management of change was required, covering the whole corporate planning process. This revolution was driven by the top manager and included the rapid mobilisation of a Programme and Project Management Environment. This capability has been honed and developed over a number of years and has provided the company with a key competitive advantage that has allowed it to sustain its market leading position.

Window on practice 1.1

A major financial services organisation experienced dramatic increases in business following the deregulation of the personal pensions market. However, the organisation could not cope with the increase and as a result orders were processed poorly. Customers and brokers became disillusioned and withdrew business from the company. The company was ranked as nineteenth out of 20 in broker satisfaction surveys and had a poor reputation in the industry. The company was firmly rooted on a 'burning platform' and needed to take radical action if it was to survive.

A new leader was appointed who set about the task of transforming the organisation. Over a period of time the organisation successfully transformed and rose from nineteenth in the satisfaction survey to first and won a coveted 'Company of the Year' award. One of the key drivers for the turnaround was the recognition for the need and development of a programme and project culture to manage the changes that had to be undertaken. The most senior manager personally championed the development of this capability. The organisation continues to thrive and has retained its market leading position built on the back of its ability to manage change in a controlled and timely way.

2
THE CHANGE IMPERATIVE

Managing change continues to present the senior management team with greater challenges than ever before. Many organisations struggle with the impact of change and find that their plans fail to materialise into benefits. Often organisations see that their carefully planned change is suddenly invalidated by an unforeseen event because their approach to change management is too inflexible to allow them to respond in a timely way.

> **Window on practice 2.1: An example of poor change control**
>
> An insurance company in the US conducted a 30-person project that took three years to complete, against an original estimate of one year. When it finished, they found that the company had stopped selling the product more than a year before.

The probability of having to make 'emergency' or contingency plans is reduced where the original plan is undertaken in a considered, structured and controlled way.

2.1 Why does change still fail?

Alarmingly, and despite the warnings and lessons learned, up to 80 per cent of all changes fail to deliver the planned benefits. Many run over time and cost and the deliverables do not match the business specification or meet management expectations. Often, the true cost of the change is not evident until the full consequences of the poor delivery are understood.

There are many reasons for failure but broadly speaking changes fail for management reasons rather than technical ones. One of the key management failings is the informal approach that some organisations take to managing change.

Ad hoc approaches rarely provide the tight structured environment required for the effective initiation and control of change.

> **Window on practice 2.2: An example of poor benefits realisation**
>
> A Scandinavian country conducted a survey into the cost–benefit analysis of projects across most of its government and found that only 16 per cent could document quantitative benefits from investments in change during the previous four years.

A number of key issues are associated with an ad hoc approach:

- A clear business justification for change may never be developed. Rather than change being determined by a formal cost–benefit–risk business appraisal, it is often the case that change is driven by a senior personality as opposed to a professional management process

- This may then be compounded with multiple change initiatives being introduced across various parts of the organisation with little or no consideration given to the organisation's capacity to absorb these changes

- Moreover, the individual changes may start by being insulated within a particular function, isolating other parts of the business from the change and the potential implications of the delivery. The full implications for the whole organisation are sometimes understood only when it is too late and the benefits realised in one part of the business are reduced or even disappear, as an unforeseen negative impact of the change becomes apparent elsewhere

- Finally, once changes are initiated they tend to be allowed to run their course regardless of external developments in the environment within which the organisation is operating. Too often this results in the delivered change being inappropriate and ineffective.

2.2   The need to manage change

Successful organisations have recognised the need to face up to change and manage it, rather than let change manage them. Change provides an opportunity to improve the status quo and deliver business benefits as a result.

Improving the status quo requires the definition and delivery of a set of unique outputs that, once applied to the existing operation, will deliver the necessary improvement in performance. Changes to the status quo will almost certainly cut across functions within the organisation, a fact that has traditionally led to problems of ownership of the changes and consequently difficulty in realising the expected benefits. Improving cross-functional 'team working' requires a new management capability built on the foundation of a controlled and professional environment. The new capability needs to bring together the various parts of the business and focus this collective strength on working together towards a common goal. Successful organisations tend to have adopted a combined programme- and project-based approach to the management of change.

2.3   How to manage change

The approach taken to manage change will depend on the nature of the change envisaged:

- Project management is suited to making tactical changes where there are closely bounded and scoped deliverables that can be relatively well defined (bounded change)

- Programme management is suited to strategic change initiatives where there are complex and changing inter-relationships in a wide, dynamic and uncertain environment (unbounded change).

Project Management is effective for delivering bounded change because all that is required is for projects to focus on the production of predefined outputs. This is because there will be a clear understanding of how these outputs will be applied to achieve the organisation's desired outcomes. Outputs are specified deliverables from projects that are delivered within time, cost, quality and scope constraints.

Whereas projects tend to be focused on delivering *outputs,* programmes are focused on achieving *outcomes.* Outcomes are the effects of change and form the vision for the programme. To achieve the desired outcomes, active management of the change process is needed. This often includes transforming behaviour, attitudes, or ways of working. Thus, in the case of unbounded change where the link between outputs and outcomes is often less clear, in addition to the focus on delivering predefined outputs, attention needs to be brought to bear on the management of:

- A portfolio of multiple projects

- The transition of the organisation to enable it to absorb multiple changes

- The realisation of measurable benefits from the outcomes delivered.

Whilst some projects may operate as stand-alone projects, Programme Management and Project Management can be regarded as complementary approaches. During a programme lifecycle, projects are initiated, executed, and closed. Programmes provide an umbrella under which these projects can be co-ordinated. The programme integrates the projects so that it can deliver an outcome greater than the sum of its parts. Programme Management does not, however, replace the need for competent project direction and management. Programmes must be underpinned by a controlled project environment of effective direction, management and delivery, and reporting disciplines that are common to all projects within the programme.

Whether we are dealing with bounded or unbounded change, chances of success are greatly improved where the change is managed through a multi-functional team, led by a professional Programme or Project Manager.

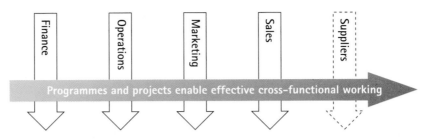

Figure 2.1 The programme and project model for effective management of change

The chances of success are improved still further where the team uses tried and tested approaches to Programme and Project Management. This reduces the overhead for the start-up of each programme or project. It also provides a framework for building associated skills and gives the senior management team the information they require to control the programme or project.

The OGC guides *Managing Successful Programmes* (MSP) and *Managing Successful Projects with PRINCE2* (PRINCE2) offer easy access to tried and tested best practice approaches to Programme and Project Management.

Am I controlling change? A simple health check

With some organisations spending the equivalent of up to 25 per cent of their annual operating budget on programmes and projects, it is vital that senior management are able to answer the following questions on a regular basis to determine whether there are appropriate controls around the changes:

- What is the budget for change?
- How many programmes and projects are running or planned?
- What is the current status of these?
- What are the precise benefits that will be delivered?
- What actual benefits have been delivered?
- Who is accountable for realising benefits?
- What are the processes for initiation and control?
- Do we have the skills to deliver the programmes and projects, now and in the future?
- Do we have the capacity to accommodate the number of changes?

Senior management need an effective mechanism to allow them to direct the resources of the organisation at the right targets. Well applied programmes and project management approaches provide the controlled environment that will allow senior management to initiate programmes and projects confidently and delegate some responsibility and authority for their management.

Tables 2.1 and 2.2 give examples of situations for managing change as a programme or project.

Table 2.2 identifies some situations where change should be managed as a project.

Table 2.1 Situations where change should be managed as a programme

Situation	Why
Where high-level policy or strategic objectives are difficult to define	To clearly specify outcomes and to break down activity into manageable portions. Particularly important for large programmes
Where there is complexity or large-scale change	To co-ordinate activities across many specialisms, business units or organisations
Where there are design interfaces between projects	To harmonise design and preserve integrity
Where resources are scarce	To set priorities and resolve conflicts. To focus on those projects and activities that will deliver the strategic objectives
Where there is the potential for common activities or products across more than one project	To identify and exploit the opportunities for efficiencies through sharing
Where there is the probability of change during the running of the programme	To provide flexible information flows and facilitate top-down, well informed decision-making so that appropriate adjustments can be made
Where there is uncertainty	To provide a framework for communication and to promote common values and shared responsibilities so as to foster collaboration from all the parties involved
Where there is the potential to deliver a series of outcomes	To realise benefits early
Where there is a requirement for overall improvement	To align and co-ordinate a range of continuous improvements to business operations and services
Where there is a high degree of risk	To manage, monitor and reduce the risk to acceptable levels without impeding the successful outcome of the programme

Table 2.2 Situations where change should be managed as a project

Situation	Why
Where the scope of the change is limited and confined within organisational boundaries	To enable a temporary organisation to be established to implement the change in a controlled manner
Where the objectives of the change in terms of business benefits are clear and understood	To focus the attention of the business on the realisation of the benefits that should result once the project has delivered its products
Where solutions are easily identified and can be translated into defined and measurable business products	To focus the attention of the project on the delivery of these products, to the required standard of quality, within the specified constraints of time, cost and scope; and that are capable of achieving the business benefits
Where there is a clear development cycle for the production of the required business products	To enable a credible plan to be developed defining the activities and resources required to create the business products

2.4 MSP – an introduction

MSP is now used extensively by the UK government and the wider public sector, and it is widely recognised and used in the private sector, both in the UK and internationally. It embodies established and proven best practice in programme management. It provides a common language for all participants in a programme and its attendant projects.

The MSP guide describes OGC's recommended approach for managing programmes. Its purpose is to explain:

- The characteristics of programmes
- The concepts of programme management
- The main roles, activities, processes and products of the approach.

Programme management is a structured framework that can help organisations deliver change. MSP provides this framework, through organisation, processes, inputs and outputs, and ways of thinking. Together, these enable talented people to manage change and cope with its inherent complexity, risks, problems and challenges.

MSP identifies four key attributes of a successful programme:

- A clear and consistent vision of the changed business or other outcome

- A focus on benefits and the internal and external threats to their achievement
- Co-ordination of a number of projects and their interdependencies in pursuit of these goals
- Leadership, influence, management and direction of the transition, including handling cultural change.

These attributes should run as continuous 'strands' throughout a programme. As such they are reflected in the leadership roles defined within MSP and the various elements of the programme information that forms the Programme Definition.

MSP consists of two main elements:

- Programme Management Principles. The concepts, strategies, techniques and tools that underpin programmes
- Programme Management Lifecycle. Consists of six processes describing the activities, inputs, outputs, decisions and responsibilities of the programme lifecycle.

2.5   PRINCE2 – an introduction

PRINCE2 is a structured project management method. It provides a set of best practice processes and is widely used within both the public and private sectors for the effective selection and management of projects. It is the recommended approach within the UK government who developed it from studies of industrial best practice.

PRINCE2 best practice processes are based on other existing project management methods and the lessons from dozens of case studies, as well as consultation with over 150 users. The diversity of organisations involved in developing the best practice processes means that PRINCE2 is highly adaptable to different project circumstances across a broad span of industries and sectors.

It provides a common understanding of key elements of a project; namely:

- How it should be organised
- When different aspects of the project will be completed
- The level of responsibility, authority and accountability held by those involved in the project
- The steps needed to guide the project through controlled, well managed and visible sets of activities to achieve the desired results.

PRINCE2 consists of three main elements:

- The PRINCE2 process model, which itself consists of eight distinctive management processes, covering the activities from setting the project off on the right track, through controlling and managing the project's progress, to the completion of the project

- Eight components, each covering a key aspect of project management, that are used by the processes

- Three techniques that may be used to support other aspects of the method. PRINCE2 offers very few techniques, preferring to leave the choice of techniques to the users of the method.

2.6   Adopting OGC best practice

Adopting MSP and/or PRINCE2 allows an organisation to avoid the drawbacks of trial and error and gain a fast track to effective programme/project management together with the benefits that come from managing change well.

Because the effective management of change is critical for survival and growth it is not enough to take a few good people from the operation and call them Programme and/or Project Managers; they need to be trained for the task. To encourage and facilitate their use, MSP and PRINCE2 are fully supported by training, accreditation and professional development structures.

Organisations may also find it useful to assess capability against one of OGC's Maturity Models which are freely available as web downloads via the OGC website. Maturity Model assessments can be used to set a baseline against which an organisation can plan and measure improvements in programme and project management over time. OGC's models are fully supported by accredited consultancy organisations.

MSP and PRINCE2 ensure that many of the issues normally associated with an ad hoc approach to change management are avoided. Table 2.3 highlights some of the key features and the associated benefits of primary importance to senior management.

Window on practice 2.3: An example of realising benefits

An international software company has realised efficiency savings in excess of $2m per annum as a direct result of their adoption of MSP and PRINCE2 in conjunction with Six Sigma as their framework for managing business change, programme and project management across global operations.

Table 2.3 The benefits of MSP and PRINCE2 to senior management

MSP/PRINCE2 Feature	Benefit
Business Case	The programme or project is justified through the development of a clear Business Case. This describes, at the outset, what the benefits are, the cost and time to produce them, and why it is worth undertaking the programme or project
Clear ownership	A clear organisation structure is defined which ensures that all parties involved in the programme or project understand roles, responsibilities and who has accountability for delivery of the benefits
Cross-functional working	An output/outcome-based focus allows the identification and scheduling of specific skills and activity
Controlled environment	<ul><li>A phased approach to the programme or project provides a number of critical control points for management. A review takes place at the end of each phase and ensures that the justification for the programme or project is still valid<ul><li>MSP breaks a programme into tranches</li><li>PRINCE2 breaks a project into stages</li></ul></li><li>Exception-based management allows senior management to delegate with confidence. Senior management can take the 'big picture' view of the programme or project and need only get involved when agreed tolerances are exceeded</li><li>Breaking the programme or project up into manageable pieces allows management to commit to one phase at a time. This allows the justification for the programme or project to be periodically reviewed at the end of each phase</li></ul>

Summary

- An organisation needs the ability to manage change well as a key driver for organisational success
- Change requires careful and skilful control
- Programme and Project Management provides the structured approach required
- MSP provides a structure and set of processes that provide the following benefits:
  - More effective delivery of changes because they can be planned and implemented in an integrated way, ensuring that current business operations are not adversely affected

- Effective response to strategic initiatives by bridging the gap between strategies and projects
- Keeping activities focused on the business change objectives by providing a framework for senior management to direct and manage the change process
- More efficient management of resources by providing a mechanism for project prioritisation and project integration
- Better management of risk because the wider context is understood and explicitly acknowledged
- Helping to achieve real business benefits through a formal process of benefit identification, management, realisation and measurement
- Improved control through a framework within which the costs of introducing new infrastructure, standards and quality regimes can be justified, measured and assessed
- Clarification of how new business operations will deliver improved performance by defining the desired benefits and linking these to the achievement of new working practices
- More effective management of the Business Case by building and maintaining a Business Case that clearly compares current business operations with the more beneficial future business operations
- More efficient co-ordination and control of the often complex range of activities by clearly defining roles and responsibilities for managing the Project Portfolio and realising the benefits expected from the programme
- Smooth transition from current to future business operations through the clear recognition and responsibility for preparing the organisation for migration to new ways of working
- Achieving a consistent system of new or amended policies, standards, and working practices through the integrated definition, planning, delivery and assurance of the required changes

- PRINCE2 provides projects with:
- A controlled and organised start, middle and end
- Regular reviews of progress against plan and against the Business Case
- Flexible decision points
- Automatic management control of any deviations from the plan
- The involvement of management and stakeholders at the right time during the project
- Good communication channels between the project management team and the rest of the organisation
- Agreement on the required quality at the outset and continuous monitoring against those requirements

- Senior managers must take a lead role. They must embrace change as an opportunity to drive performance. They must achieve this by becoming the active champions of the **Programme and Project Management Environment.**

Chapter 3, *Realising the big picture*, looks at the key role a Programme and Project Management Environment plays in achieving an organisation's business strategy.

3
REALISING THE BIG PICTURE

Having noted that an effective change capability is critical to the organisation's survival and future success, this section demonstrates why a reliable Programme and Project Management Environment is central to the successful translation of strategy into operational changes.

Figure 3.1 shows the inter-relationship between the four organisation levels of strategies, programmes, projects and operations, where:

- **Business strategies**, initiatives or policies are influenced and shaped from both the internal and the external business environment

- **Programmes** are then defined, scoped and prioritised to implement and deliver the outcome(s) required from those strategies, initiatives or policies

- Programmes, in turn, initiate, monitor and align the **projects** and related activities that are needed to create new products or service capabilities, or to effect changes in business operations

- The projects will deliver and implement the required outputs into business **operations**, until, finally, the full benefits of the programme can be realised

- **Operations** may also initiate stand-alone **projects** in response to local problems and opportunities.

By looking at strategic change empirically, the context and argument for MSP and PRINCE2 and how to deploy them effectively can clearly be seen. Too often organisations attempt to 'bolt on' some new capability where it is either inappropriate or where the fundamental conditions for it to operate successfully do not exist.

3.1 Business strategy

Organisations need to anticipate and deliver the future needs of their stakeholders and clients (as opposed to constantly being in reactive mode as the environment around them changes). The key capabilities are:

3.1.1 Strategy Definition

- Insight into the future opportunities and threats in the environment in which the organisation operates

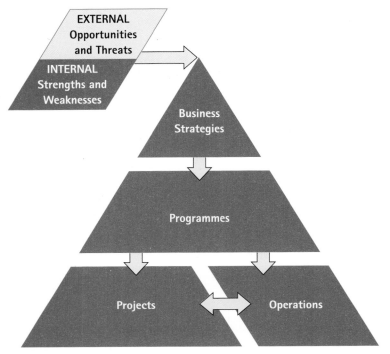

Figure 3.1 Inter-relationship between strategies, programmes, projects and operations

- The ability to anticipate the needs and expectations of an organisation's stakeholders and clients in this future state
- The ability to define the organisation's response as a linked set of strategic objectives, critical success factors and strategic Key Performance Indicators (KPIs)
- The ability to define innovative yet achievable future propositions which will deliver value to stakeholders, clients and partners
- The ability to plan an achievable set of actions to deliver the strategy.

3.1.2 Strategy Implementation

- The ability to align operations, programmes and projects with strategic objectives
- The ability to initiate the right set of strategic programmes
- The discipline to keep programmes, projects and operations aligned and to realise the expected benefits.

Having only one of these capabilities is not enough. A winning strategy will not benefit an organisation that is incapable of translating it into meaningful action. On the other hand, being able to implement the wrong strategy quickly is another recipe for failure.

3.1.3 Strategy Definition – creating the 'big picture'

A well-defined strategy defines the overall target operating model required to achieve the organisation's aspirations. It is this integrated 'big picture' that provides the map of where the organisation is going and what it will feel like for the employees and clients when they get there.

If the target operation represents 'where we want to be', then the current operation can be assessed and analysed in the same terms in order to understand 'where we are now' (see Figure 3.2). However, care needs to be exercised to avoid 'analysis paralysis' in terms of the current operation and indeed such an analysis may not be required at all for some transformational changes or new ventures.

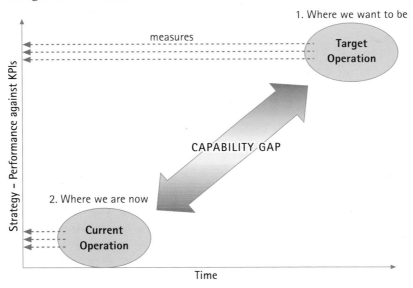

Figure 3.2 'Big picture' view – current and target operating models

3.1.4 Strategic planning

Having modelled the desired future state, strategic planning identifies the set of actions required to migrate from the current operation to the target operation. This is the crucial test of the feasibility of the strategy. There may need to be a number of iterations, reworking the strategy and plans until a challenging but credible outcome is achieved. The resulting strategic plan

- Describes how the 'target operation' will be achieved through a co-ordinated set of programmes and/or projects
- Is supported by a refocusing of operational plans (see Figure 3.3).

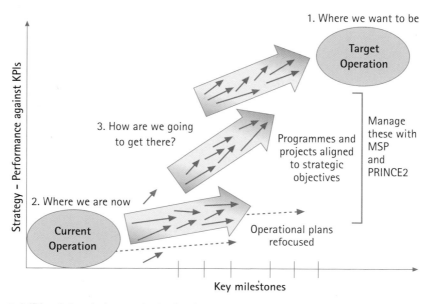

Figure 3.3 'Big picture' view – strategic plan

If the language of 'required capabilities' is used, then auditable links can be maintained between the strategy and the programmes and attendant projects required to deliver the strategic objectives. In a controlled Programme and Project Management Environment there is a clear focus on the delivery of these capabilities via project deliverables. A key principle of MSP is the distinction between outcomes and outputs. Programmes are designed to produce outcomes which are the results of change and can be quantified as benefits. A key principle of PRINCE2 is the focus on products or outputs rather than activity. When applied in the operation these products provide new capabilities (e.g. improved client service via the Internet).

The planning activity needs to be informed by a real understanding of the organisation's ability and capacity to change. A common approach is to use the numbers and skill levels of a core group of people as an indicator (e.g. Project Managers, IT professionals). A more comprehensive set of indicators is available only when the organisation manages its programmes and projects in a controlled and disciplined environment, such as with MSP and PRINCE2, in which past performance can be understood.

20

3.2 Aligning programme/project and operational plans with strategy

The big picture view provides a powerful mechanism for understanding how activities must be aligned and resources co-ordinated to ensure that the organisation moves in the right direction at the right speed. The key issue is balancing the needs of the 'business as usual' operation with the need for strategic change. Figure 3.4 illustrates the close alignment required.

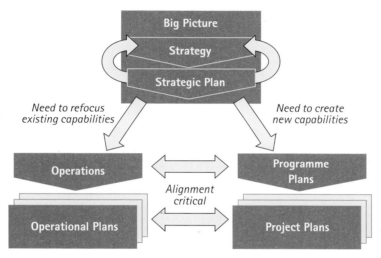

Figure 3.4 Aligning programme/project and operational plans with strategy

Alignment with strategy can only be maintained through joined-up management and a disciplined approach to managing change. If strategy is loosely connected or just expressed as an ambiguous set of aspirations, the organisation will struggle to do the right thing in programmes, projects and in the operations. In this situation people attempt to fill the vacuum with their own interpretation of where the organisation should be going, which at best wastes resources and at worst moves the organisation in the wrong direction.

When strategic alignment is working, there is a clear understanding of the outcome required of the programme and each project will have its scope clearly set in terms of the capabilities it will deliver across the different elements of the operating model (e.g. product and service propositions, business processes, organisation structures, people, systems and infrastructure).

One of the key principles of MSP is the definition of the end-goal of the programme in terms of a Vision Statement and a Blueprint, with a review of the programme's performance at the end of each tranche. One of the key principles of PRINCE2 is the tight definition of project scope and verification at the end of every stage that the scope is still the same and also still valid. These principles constitute the kind of integrated management approach that optimises control and the chance of success.

3.2.1 Managing the portfolio of strategic programmes and non-strategic projects

In the real world an organisation's change agenda does not consist only of the well structured set of strategic programmes that has been defined by the top-down planning process. Strategic planning and the subsequent management of the overall portfolio of change need to acknowledge the other projects which will run in parallel with strategic programmes.

These might include changes to respond to new legislation, incremental operational improvements or routine renewal of infrastructure. Most organisations wish to do more than they have the resources to deliver, so resources need to target the areas of greatest return on investment. To achieve this, a clear process is needed to develop a Business Case for each proposed change. The compatible approaches to the Business Case in MSP and PRINCE2 mean that effective prioritisation is possible.

3.2.2 Moving into Strategy Implementation

This section has described how Strategy Definition should determine the right set of programmes and projects to achieve the organisation's strategy. The next describes the critical success factors for Strategy Implementation, focusing on what constitutes an effective Programme and Project Management Environment.

3.3 The Programme and Project Management Environment and Operational Management Capability

The critical success factors for implementing strategic change and realising the benefits are:

- An effective Programme and Project Management Environment as the key tool for the delivery of the organisation's strategic change agenda
- Sound Operational Management Capability to deliver the day-to-day business.

For organisations to achieve maximum benefit from strategic change they must excel in the management of both programmes and projects and day-to-day operations. Figure 3.5 shows the two sets of capabilities that must be balanced and aligned.

Operational Management Capability	Programme and Project Management Environment
• Ability to deliver the organisation's business as usual efficiently and effectively. • Client outcomes being achieved consistently well. • Effective operational management and control mechanisms in place. • Deployment of existing capabilities fully aligned with strategic objectives.	• Ability to deliver the new capabilities the organisation needs efficiently and effectively. • Ability to mobilise highly motivated cross-functional teams to deliver full solutions. • Effective programme and project management and co-ordination mechanisms in place. • Programme outcome and project deliverables aligned to strategic objectives.

Figure 3.5 Critical success factors for effective strategic change

This balance is critical as illustrated by the following scenarios:

3.3.1 Operational Management Capability without an effective Programme and Project Management Environment

- Power lies mainly in the current operation

- Change is resisted

- People see no benefit in taking part in programmes or projects

- Change is seen as an externally driven event

- Programmes fail to engage the key stakeholders on whom benefits realisation depends

- Projects start up with unclear goals, objectives and scope; and benefits are not quantified

- Implementation of change is painful and difficult

- Programmes and projects fail.

Organisations at this end of the spectrum might include long established companies operating in traditionally stable markets, public sector bodies which have not been restructured for many years, or organisations which have never regarded change as a core discipline (and may have always farmed out major changes to external suppliers and/or consultants).

3.3.2 Good Programme and Project Management Environment but no effective Operational Management Capability

- Change is imposed on a submissive operation
- People in the operation are collectively unable to articulate their requirements
- The means of operating the deliverables is not defined in the requirements or the specifications
- Operational impacts of changes are not understood; solution designs are fatally flawed
- Changes delivered by projects do not stick because there is no effective process management in the operation
- Benefits are not realised.

Examples of organisations fitting this description might include start-up companies who have continued with a dominant programme/project mentality or organisations which have been subjected to radical restructuring (e.g. acquisition or merger) for whom a stable business operation has yet to be re-established.

3.3.3 Neither a good Programme and Project Management Environment nor an effective Operational Management Capability

Organisations without either of these competencies are probably incapable of strategic change and are unlikely to survive in a changing business environment.

3.3.4 The winning formula – Programme and Project Management Environment, Operational Management Capability and alignment between the two

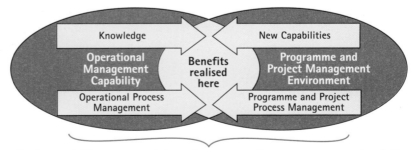

Deployment of key resources balanced across operations, programmes and projects

Figure 3.6 Operational Management Capability and Programme and Project Management Environment fully aligned

Organisations with the right balance and alignment between Programme and Project Management Environment and Operational Management Capability are well placed to achieve their strategic ambitions. This winning scenario can be characterised as follows:

- Change is seen as 'business as usual'

- Operational people feel that they have a stake in the programmes/projects being undertaken (i.e., 'It's being done by us or for us; not to us')

- Programme and project people feel they have a stake in the success of the changed operation they are delivering (i.e., 'We will be operating this after implementation')

- People who can facilitate cross-functional working are highly valued

- People move easily between Operational and Programme/Project domains

- The focus is on outcomes and benefits realisation

- Change to the operation is smooth and is scheduled to minimise disruption

- Redesigned business processes are implemented into a well managed operational environment in which compliance with the new working practices can be monitored

- Programmes/Projects and Operations agree about how benefits will be realised and by whom

- Operations start the process of benefits realisation early, in the confidence that new capabilities will be delivered as planned (e.g. allowing natural wastage of staff in areas where headcount reductions will be possible once new systems are delivered)

- Operational knowledge is fed effectively into programmes/projects at the right times (e.g. requirements definition, business process design, acceptance testing).

3.4   Critical elements of an effective Programme and Project Management Environment

Having established the key dependency on the organisation's Operational Management Capability, what constitutes an effective Programme and Project Management Environment can now be set out in detail and the benefits of MSP and PRINCE2 illustrated in this context.

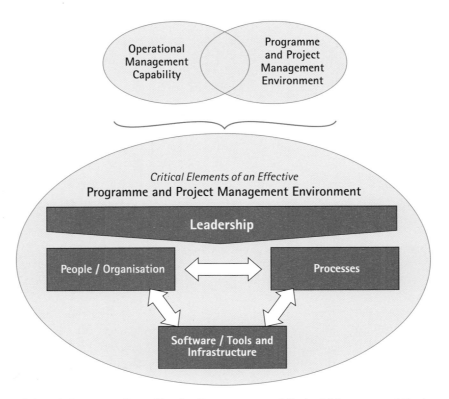

Figure 3.7 Critical elements of an effective Programme and Project Management Environment

As Figure 3.7 illustrates, an effective Programme and Project Management Environment depends on

- the right programme and project processes,
- being performed by the right people,
- deployed within the right organisational structures,
- supported by the right software tools and infrastructure,
- in the context of clear top-down leadership providing the discipline to conduct programmes and projects consistently in the right way.

If any one of these elements is weak or missing then an effective Programme and Project Management Environment cannot be said to be in place.

The next sections take each element in turn, describing why it is critical, identifying its key attributes and indicating where and how MSP and PRINCE2 deliver against each one.

3.4.1 Leadership

An effective Programme and Project Management Environment can only be sustained if there is clear leadership from the top of the organisation. It is critical that everyone understands what attitudes and behaviours are most valued by senior management and are aware of the authority and priority given to the change agenda. The objective is to achieve real focus, alignment and discipline; harnessing people's energy to achieve maximum benefit; and taking friction and wasted time out of the change process. MSP and PRINCE2's evolution and best practice status is totally compatible with this objective. They set the pattern for behaviour from top to bottom within programmes and projects. This will help to create the appropriate culture within which change can be actively managed.

This leadership is critical within the organisation, and it also communicates an important message about the organisation's change capability to stakeholders, clients and strategic partners (current and potential). It will build confidence in the organisation's ability to anticipate and respond to whatever opportunities and threats emerge in the environment it operates in and to maintain its capacity and capability to change through effective prioritisation. Benefits will accrue in terms of the ongoing support and investment of stakeholders and increased propensity of other players to partner with the organisation.

To provide the leadership required the senior team need to show a real understanding of why the Programme and Project Management Environment is critical and the controlled environment is necessary. Their consistent message should emphasise the constancy of change and the need to master it, underlining the role of the Programme and Project Management Environment in this process. The organisation will reap benefits in the following ways if the message is clear:

- ability to implement change quickly and efficiently
- ability to co-ordinate a complex change portfolio
- smooth implementation into the operational environment
- ability to continuously improve change process
- flexibility in deploying resources across programmes and projects
- ability to all 'speak the same language' in describing programmes and projects
- ability to work as one team regardless of functional boundaries, with a willing exchange of information
- ability to monitor and measure in a consistent way and make the right decisions on prioritisation and commitment of resources.

These key messages are best communicated by a combination of formal rules and a set of senior management attitudes and behaviours that help create the environment within which the principles embodied by the rules will be applied.

Rules

There should not be a bureaucratic rule book but between four and six high-level statements that make the expected set of behaviours quite clear. For example:

'No programme moves beyond identification without a Programme Brief being approved by the Sponsoring Group.'

'No project moves into its next stage without the Project Initiation Document being reviewed by the Project Board.'

This clear set of rules must be visible and acted upon throughout the organisation. They should be set in the context of an overall environment that ensures they are universally perceived as common sense. It is not enough for programmes and projects to go through the motions when using particular programme and project management approaches, but an environment should be established where everyone abides by the basic rules without question. Creative energies should focus on the business issues at hand rather than on debating the relative merits of different programme and project management approaches.

It is important that these rules are seen to come from the senior management rather than from the organisation's specialist programme or project management group (or one department which may have been early adopters of formal programme or project management disciplines).

The senior team's attitudes and behaviours

The ways in which the senior management team can build an effective Programme and Project Management Environment vary from organisation to organisation. Typically, however, these actions and attitudes make a real difference:

- Communicate a clear statement of intent that all significant change must be managed within the controlled Programme and Project Management Environment
- Ensure there is close integration of strategic, programme, project and operational planning
- Acknowledge and reward the champions of change within the organisation
- Endorse the informal community of Programme and Project Managers and support their development through MSP and PRINCE2 training

- Demonstrate the importance of the programme and project management principles and rules through leading by example (for instance, no exceptions for 'pet' projects). MSP and PRINCE2 will reinforce the desired behaviour as, for example, programmes and projects can only be progressed where they have a sound business justification

- Actively engage in resolving programme and project issues quickly if they have correctly been escalated to senior management level

- Support and empower the people who take the initiative to establish cross-functional mechanisms and lines of communication. MSP and PRINCE2 enables senior management to manage by exception and therefore to delegate much of the day-to-day control of programmes and projects with confidence

- Welcome real messages about programme and project progress and issues; encourage transparency and openness

- Be active in the Programme and Project Management Environment, take part in programme and project events and communications, visiting and contributing to programmes and projects (i.e. not just 'royal visits')

- Adopt the common language of the Programme and Project Management Environment and insist on its use whenever appropriate

- Actively monitor formal reporting against programme and project objectives. MSP and PRINCE2 uses the Sponsoring Group and Project Board respectively as a key mechanism for reporting that allows senior management to have clear visibility of progress and issues and therefore the control that is required

- Operations management should actively engage in programmes and projects; they should encourage and reward the contribution of their people to programme and project success

- Demonstrate and encourage cross-functional behaviour

- Give equal weight to programme and/or project needs and operational and/or functional needs when deciding on resource allocation

- Sustain a feeling of energy and enthusiasm around the change agenda

- Support and encourage internal communications regarding successful programmes and projects

- Encourage lessons to be learned, circulated and capitalised upon

- Manage the balance between all elements of the Programme and Project Management Environment, investing in the people, process and tool elements as appropriate, as failure to manage the balance can cause a programme or project to lose focus and go off track.

3.4.2 Processes

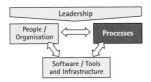

Programme and Project Management processes represent what is actually done in practice – how the organisation defines, initiates and executes programmes and projects. They are the real backbone of an effective Programme and Project Management Environment and should embody the high-level rules and principles being communicated by the senior management through their leadership. MSP and PRINCE2 provide senior management with the conditions that they need to provide effective leadership through the clear definition of the senior management roles and responsibilities and of the processes and organisation required. For example, the role of the Programme and Project Boards allows the senior managers of the principal and partner organisations to work collaboratively and truly understand the progress of the programme or project, and to make effective decisions based on accurate and timely information.

A good set of programme and project management processes will consistently achieve predictable and measurable outcomes. It is important that each programme and project management process is understood in the following terms:

- What is its overall objective?
- Who are its key stakeholders?
- What outcomes does each stakeholder need from the process?
- How will we measure that each outcome has been achieved?
- What outputs and/or products will achieve each outcome?
- What quality criteria should be applied to each output?
- What activities are needed to produce these outputs?
- What resources are required to carry out the activities?
- What knowledge and other inputs are required?
- What is the role and responsibility of senior management?

By asking and answering the above questions not only at the outset but at every progress point throughout the programme or project, MSP and PRINCE2 ensure that the objective remains in focus at all times. Each process should be defined and communicated in such a way that it is quite clear what is expected each time the process is carried out.

Formal process management disciplines should be applied to the programme and project processes. These include explicit process ownership, performance measurement and mechanisms for continuous improvement such as process mapping and re-engineering. This will ensure that processes do not become fixed and that they reflect the times and current technology. New practices or changes from the accepted practice should still be sanctioned and assessed, but via pilot exercises rather than by renegade programmes or projects unilaterally deciding to do things differently.

There is real benefit in the community of Programme and Project Managers taking a leading role in the ongoing development of programme and project management processes, regardless of whether Programme and Project Managers are drawn from a single specialist group or a virtual pool from around the organisation. By monitoring and recording programmes' and projects' performance of their processes the strategic planning function can build a realistic view of the organisation's change capability and inform the estimating of costs and benefits for future programmes and projects.

The need for formal programme and project management approaches

Ideally processes should be:

- Repeatable
- Predictable
- Managed
- Measurable
- Controllable.

To achieve this, a set of managed materials defining the task breakdowns, products, and roles that make up the process is necessary. These templates and route maps should represent the collective experience of the organisation in running programmes and projects, reflecting best practice built up over the years. They should be accompanied by a user's guide explaining when some elements must be used, and recommending the optional use of others, guiding staff towards the best way to achieve all the required outcomes of the programme and project processes.

Many organisations short-cut the creation of this knowledge base by adopting MSP and PRINCE2 which are themselves best practice and can provide the core for the organisation's programme and project management processes. Section 3.5 describes in detail how MSP and PRINCE2 do this.

To summarise the case for pursuing programme and project management and, in particular, MSP and PRINCE2:

Benefits of formal programme and project management approaches

- Creation of a common language to improve communication
- Consistent execution of programme and project processes

- Reduction in non-value-added time in and around programmes and projects
- Programmes and projects can concentrate on the business issues at hand rather than reinventing programme and/or project processes.

Additional benefits of adopting market leading non-proprietary approaches

Organisations are increasingly involved in change initiatives that go beyond their own boundaries, within the context of alliances and partnerships. Because MSP and PRINCE2 are market-leading approaches the following additional benefits accrue and the organisation is able to:

- Engage external resources (e.g. contractors, new employees) who already 'speak the language', understand what is required, and can therefore become productive members of the team quickly

- Partner with other organisations in joint ventures with reduced friction and faster collaborative working

- Select third-party suppliers to execute programmes or projects on the organisation's behalf without sacrificing the benefits of the established Programme and Project Management Environment

- Benchmark externally and drive up performance.

3.4.3 People and organisation

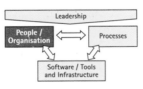

An effective Programme and Project Management Environment ultimately consists of a critical mass of people with the right skills, attitudes and behaviours. These are not just the people working in programme and project teams, but also those in operations, functional specialists and people in all other parts of the organisation. It is a mistake to neglect the 'people' part of the equation in favour of programme and project management methods and tools. This can happen because the 'soft' people issues are seen as more difficult and time-consuming.

It is not enough for the senior management to endorse a set of programme and project management principles and invest in programme and project management processes and tools; they also need to create an extended team of people who are prepared to 'live' the Programme and Project Management Environment. The challenge of strategic change demands positive attitudes and energy around the change agenda, both within programmes and projects and across the whole organisation.

This section considers the issues relating to individuals within the Programme and Project Management Environment (**people**) and then goes on to examine the context that must be created for them to work in (**organisation**).

People

It is critical that the Programme and Project Management Environment lives in the hearts and minds of the individuals within the organisation. The quality of a change capability is embodied in the individuals within operational and programme/project domains in step with the strategic aims of the organisation. This can only be achieved through the alignment, competency, and attitudes of individuals and their programme/project management skills.

These are examples of the skills and behaviours that should be highly valued:

- People who contribute to programmes and projects with both discipline and common sense, channelling their energy and enthusiasm through the agreed processes
- People who are fully focused on programme and project objectives but are at the same time sensitive to operational needs
- People who are fully focused on operational objectives but are at the same time supportive of programme and project imperatives
- People who can facilitate cross-functional working
- People who build their careers through success in both operational and programme/project roles
- People on programmes and projects who apply programme/project management disciplines at all times regardless of their own role (i.e. not leaving these disciplines to be externally applied by the people in 'Programme/Project Manager' or 'Programme/Project Office' roles)
- Specialists who can communicate and work effectively with others (rather than adopting a defensive attitude of 'knowledge is power')
- People on programmes and projects who take the initiative in managing relationships with the programme/project's stakeholders.

To achieve this, the mechanisms for aligning people's behaviour must be correctly tuned, for example:

Career paths

In organisations without a real Programme and Project Management Environment, stepping out of an operational role to join a programme or project can turn out to be a bad career move. The individual can be out of sight and out of mind as far as career progression is concerned, or worse still may find that there is no operational role to go back to when the programme or project is finished.

Talented people should be encouraged to move between operational and programme/project roles and their career progression should match the value they add in both domains. It is in the organisation's interest to have people who understand both programmes/projects and operations. The incentives should be in place to encourage this, ideally reinforced by high-profile role models.

Recognition and rewards

In a healthy Programme and Project Management Environment success in operational and programme/project roles is equally weighted and performance management processes fairly assess the contributions people make in both arenas. Furthermore, the rewards and recognition for people who have stepped out of a role in order to take on a challenge in a programme or project should match both the contribution they have made and the risk they have taken in leaving the 'comfort zone'.

Professional development

Support for formal training and accreditation in programme and project management disciplines can provide an important statement of intent for the organisation. This should not be confined to a specialist group of Programme and Project Managers but should be extended to all people who could have a significant bearing on the success of programmes or projects in different roles (e.g. Programme Senior Responsible Owners, Business Change Managers and Project Board Members). To encourage mobility between operational areas and programmes/projects, as recommended above, operational managers are key candidates for programme and project management training. MSP and PRINCE2 provide users with an extensive range of training and consultancy services to assist with the mapping of a programme and project management career path and the training and accreditation of the team.

Organisation

The way programmes and projects are organised and configured to interact with the rest of the organisation can make an important contribution to the overall Programme and Project Management Environment. This section considers organisation in and around individual programmes and projects.

How individual programmes and projects are organised

The organisation of each individual programme and project must reflect the alignment between it and its key stakeholders; in particular the operational areas where benefits will be realised. The programme or project must not be a closed entity (except where the need for confidentiality overrides this). MSP and PRINCE2 emphasise transparency and communication with the rest of the organisation, providing for this by ensuring effective communication.

Communication mechanisms

Effective two-way communication between programmes and projects and the wider organisation is important. This could be achieved through a number of mechanisms including open programme/project rooms, open days, brainstorm and review, 'Post-it note' sessions and touring roadshows as well as the more conventional bulletins in newsletters or on the Intranet.

The objective is to allow programmes and projects to benefit from the collective knowledge of the whole organisation as well as to promote preparedness and anticipation in the community affected by the changes.

Programme and project stakeholders

In addition to this broad campaign to raise awareness and readiness, targeted and formally managed activities should communicate with specific stakeholders of the programme or project (areas and individuals within areas). There may be specific relationship objectives defined for individual stakeholders and people within the programme or project are specifically accountable for achieving these objectives. The aim is to keep significant areas and individuals involved and engaged so that the programme or project can succeed.

Figure 3.8 illustrates this set of relationships between the programmes and projects and their stakeholders.

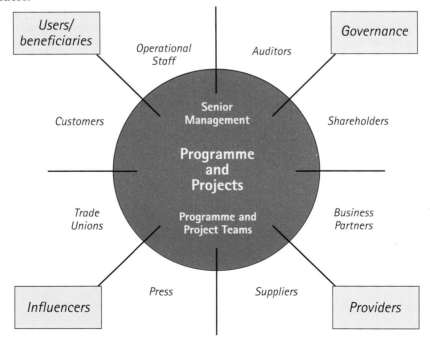

Figure 3.8 Programme and project stakeholders

3.4.4 Software tools and infrastructure

Having the right tools and infrastructure significantly improves the chances of an effective Programme and Project Management Environment being sustained. Some might argue that for larger organisations the necessary consistency and control is not possible without significant automation of programme and/or project processes and communication mechanisms. Nevertheless, tools in particular need to be selected and applied with focus and discipline so that they truly enable programme and/or project processes (rather than forcing the use of practices inconsistent with the Programme and Project Management Environment). In the diagram used throughout this section it is significant that 'software tools and infrastructure' is shown at the bottom, with a supporting role in relation to 'people/organisation' and 'processes'. It would be a mistake to try to build the Programme and Project Management Environment by starting with the selection of a set of software tools. Only when the required programme and project processes are in place, being performed by people with the right attitudes and behaviours, are the conditions right for tools to be introduced in a disciplined way to support what they are trying to achieve.

> **Window on practice 3.1**
>
> A company invested in three different project management toolsets in five years, each time hoping that use of the new toolset would create a consistent and disciplined project environment. Eventually it was accepted that the issue was the culture into which the tools were being introduced and this was addressed in a top-down manner.
>
> The right software tools and infrastructure can, however, make a significant contribution to the Programme and Project Management Environment.

Software tools

There is a long history of PC-based tools that support programme and project planning and resource scheduling and techniques like critical path analysis. Careful use of these is clearly beneficial provided the information is not confined to the computer screen and detailed reports. It is often more important to have large visible diagrams that groups of people can debate and understand together, even if some of the intricate detail is not visible. Carrying out slick automatic task rescheduling on a PC package does not in itself realign large numbers of people with a change in plans.

Other well established uses of software tools include:

- Shared programme or project repositories with support for document version control and/or configuration management

- Enabling of programme and project processes through groupware (e.g. Lotus Notes)
- Hypertext-style automation of programme and project management documentation
- Communication of programme and project status information via an Intranet.

More recent innovations include

- Use of an integrated programme, project and/or operational knowledge base for impact analysis, scenario testing etc.
- Collaborative working across organisational boundaries using Internet technologies.

'Low-tech' tools

Whilst new technologies always seem to offer the hope of breakthrough improvements in productivity and quality, it is often the case that simpler tools are better suited to the sort of Programme and Project Management Environment described in this section:

- Brown paper and 'Post-it notes' to enable fast, collaborative brainstorming of programme and/or project dependencies
- Programme and/or project schedules on large posters
- Big charts showing the deliverables for a programme and/or project team, with spaces to tick completed steps.

Infrastructure

Programme and project accommodation, equipment and information can also reinforce the principles of the Programme and Project Management Environment in a number of ways. These are over and above the normal hygiene factors of decent working spaces and facilities. Examples include:

- Programme and project 'war rooms' with key progress information all around the walls, where people come together to monitor progress and manage issues
- Programme and project communication areas with open-door policy
- Mock-ups of the future operational environment; the people who will use the new facility to be delivered can come here and see simulations of what it will be like
- Space allocated to programmes and projects for large-scale brainstorming and communication sessions
- Communication infrastructures to support efficient collaborative working between dispersed groups (e.g. videoconferencing)
- Access to relevant data and information sources.

Appropriate use of these types of facilities can deliver significant benefits but may also incur significant cost. Therefore making provision for them is tangible proof of an organisation's commitment to the Programme and Project Management Environment.

3.4.5 The overall Programme and Project Management Environment

In addition to the positive ways in which individual programmes and projects can be configured, there are a number of factors relating to the overall environment within which programmes and projects take place that can contribute to the right Programme and Project Management Environment. Examples include:

- An environment where it is natural for operational areas to lend good people to programmes and projects. This is easier where the programme and project management approaches are widely known and used

- Fluidity in the way people move from programme/project to operational roles and vice versa

- A vigorous informal community of programme and project management people enabling continuous improvement of the resource pool and communication of best practice

- Programme and project roles understood and valued (e.g. Business Change Manager and Senior User)

- Authority is known and accepted, and is based more on appropriate skills and competence than on 'grade'

- Formal ownership of programme and project management processes

- Acceptance of the guiding programme and project management principles which are applied without heavy bureaucracy, and are not seen as being imposed from outside by programme and/or project management specialists

- People across the organisation do not just go through the motions with regard to the rules of the Programme and Project Management Environment

- People genuinely understand the required outcomes of programme and project processes rather than following a task list without really appreciating the purpose

- An overall confidence and self-belief in the organisation's own Programme and Project Management Environment (i.e. it is not undermined by external suppliers proposing to bring in their own programme and/or project management approach).

3.5 How MSP and PRINCE2 support the creation of an effective Programme and Project Management Environment

Figure 3.9 illustrates how MSP and PRINCE2 cover all the key components that make up the controlled Programme and Project Management Environment, thus providing an effective approach to programme and project management and a foundation for the management and delivery of successful change.

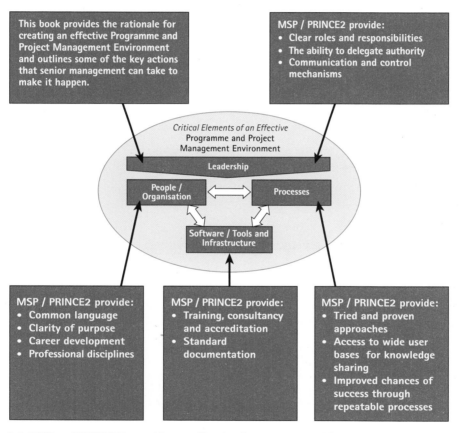

Figure 3.9 MSP and PRINCE2 provide an effective Programme and Project Management Environment

A key concept of both MSP and PRINCE2 is that they clearly differentiate between

- the management of the development process, and
- the development process itself.

This is an important benefit as it allows the organisation to focus on the change it needs to make and not waste valuable effort on understanding the programme and project management process for delivering it. Through the use of the common MSP and PRINCE2 terminology, the organisation can avoid fruitless debate about, for example, the precise definition and content of a Business Case. It is far more valuable that the organisation uses its energy and resources to understand the precise nature of the business change in the context of its own business and the design of the solution delivered by the change.

As mentioned earlier, the adoption of MSP and PRINCE2 also provides organisations with a fast track to creating an effective Programme and Project Management Environment.

Summary

- Programmes and projects provide the bridge between strategic intent and the realisation of that intent at the operational level
- Prior to initiating programmes and/or projects organisations need to have a clearly defined business strategy supported by a strategic plan
- The strategic plan needs to be aligned to the organisation's programme/project plans and the operational plans
- The critical success factors for implementing strategic change and realising the benefits are:
  - An effective Programme and Project Management Environment
  - Sound Operational Management Capability
- The critical elements of the Programme and Project Management Environment are:
  - Leadership
  - People/organisation
  - Processes
  - Software/tools and infrastructure
- The combined elements of MSP and PRINCE2 provide and support many of these critical elements and provide organisations with a fast track to creating an effective Programme and Project Management Environment.

4
MSP

Chapter 3 summarised the role of programmes and projects in translating strategy into meaningful actions. This included an overview of MSP as a proven programme management approach. This chapter identifies how MSP facilitates the co-ordinated organisation, direction and implementation of a portfolio of projects and describes the benefits.

4.1 Overview

A key principle of MSP is that for a programme to be successful it must focus on four critical success factors. These are:

- A clear and consistent **Vision** of the changed business or other outcome:
    - A programme typically involves significant change across many strands of business operation and potentially across more than one organisation. It may also involve change to individuals, groups or services that are outside the organisation. A clearly defined vision for the change will ensure there is a good understanding of what must be designed and delivered so that the desired outcomes can be achieved
    - The changed business is described within MSP by the use of two separate but complementary documents:

    The Vision Statement. This is an outward-facing description of the new capabilities resulting from the programme delivery. It will describe the new services, improved service levels or innovative ways of working with customers

    The Blueprint. This is a model of the business or organisation, its working practices and processes, the information it requires and the technology that will be needed to deliver the capability described in the Vision Statement. It describes the people, processes, information and technology capability in the new or future 'state' that will be capable of realising the benefits expected and achieving the outcomes desired.

- Co-ordination of a number of projects and their interdependencies:
    - Successful Programme Management requires careful delineation of project boundaries and outputs, rigorous identification and management of inter-project dependencies, and a clear understanding of programme versus project responsibilities. Programme Management needs to focus on the bigger picture and should not take over the responsibilities of project management. However, clear

direction should be agreed with the projects and regular reviews held to verify continual alignment to the programme objectives and plans

- The projects within the programme are grouped into a number of **tranches** each representing a distinct step change in capability and benefit delivery. The end of each tranche provides an opportunity to review benefits and assess the overall progress of the programme.

- Leadership, influence, management and direction of the **transition**, including handling cultural change:

  - Managing the transition involves planning changes, preparing for their implementation, and then implementing them. The transition process should ensure business as usual is maintained while change is happening

  - Over the life of a programme, there will be many individuals and groups who have an interest or involvement in its activities, or are affected by its outcomes. These are the programme's stakeholders

  - By their nature, programmes will inevitably change the way the organisation or business works, and this may include changing its culture and style. The objective throughout is to minimise 'stress' to the business by anticipating the magnitude of any change and allowing sufficient time and resource for the organisation to adapt. Some programmes may seek to change the activities or behaviour of people outside the organisation. The level of change will differ from programme to programme – from gaining new skills and knowledge across the workforce to deeper organisational change involving processes, behaviours and values.

- A focus on **benefits** and the internal and external threats to their achievement:

  - Beneficial change is the primary objective of any programme. Managing benefits from identification through to realisation takes time, costs money, and consumes resource, but it is vital to retain an explicit, frequently revisited focus on the intended benefits of the programme so that it remains aligned with its desired outcome.

Only by giving equal attention to each of these critical success factors can a realistic Business Case for the programme be constructed. The Business Case enables senior management to validate the ongoing viability of the programme by pulling together information relating to the benefits of the programme and the risks to achieving them, the costs and the timescales. It should be reviewed regularly throughout the programme to ensure that the programme is still affordable, still achievable, still providing value for money, and that the programme's portfolio of projects is still the appropriate and optimum way of achieving the desired outcome.

The programme's Business Case is likely to recommend an approach whereby the overall change is delivered through a series of incremental step changes achieved progressively during the life of a programme, rather than taking the very risky 'big bang' approach. In this case the programme's schedule of projects will be divided into a number of tranches, where each tranche represents a set of projects that delivers one of these step changes in capability and enables benefit realisation. These tranches also provide useful review points that assess benefit realisation and reassess the ongoing viability of the programme's Business Case.

Programmes are established to deliver the right benefits and outcomes from change, where outcomes are the effects of change and form the vision for the programme. To achieve these outcomes active management and leadership of the change process is needed. MSP proposes a programme organisation that provides for empowered decision-making, visible commitment and authority and relevant skills and experience. Whilst this organisation will engage key stakeholders the nature of programmes means that there will be many individuals or group who will be interested in, involved with or affected by the programme. MSP recognises the critical importance of engaging with these varied stakeholders throughout the life of the programme.

4.2   Lifecycle and principles

MSP describes the programme lifecycle in the form of a series of processes that cover the activities, input, outputs, decisions and responsibilities of the programme lifecycle. In defining processes it is normal to represent them in a linear format; however, each of the MSP processes is likely to require more than one iteration before the next one is begun; and having progressed to a later process it is often necessary to return to work of an earlier process for clarification or refinement of ideas and information.

During the lifecycle key management products are created. These products capture and maintain information about the programme and how it is progressing and are essential for the effective governance of the programme. This information evolves during the lifecycle of the programme:

- The **Programme Mandate** is the trigger for the programme and provides the high-level strategic objectives of the programme

- From the Programme Mandate the objectives are developed into the **Programme Brief** that provides an outline Vision Statement and Business Case for the programme. The Programme Brief in turn provides the basis for the development of:

  - The **Programme Definition**, a collection of information defining what the programme is going to deliver, how it will do it, what benefits to expect, who will be involved, and how much investment will be required

  - The **Programme, Benefits Realisation and Communication Plans,** which are used to plan, monitor and control these three important aspects of the programme

  - The **Strategies for Programme Governance,** covering quality, stakeholders, issues, risks, benefits, resources and planning and control

  - The **Risk and Issue Logs** which are used to support the ongoing management of the programme.

In addition to the lifecycle processes and management products, MSP describes the concepts, strategies, techniques and tools that underpin a programme. These are collectively known as the programme management principles. Each principle describes concepts that apply throughout the programme lifecycle.

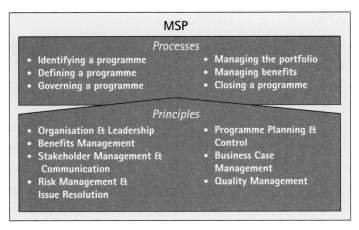

Figure 4.1 MSP processes and principles

Figure 4.1 shows the programme management processes and the principles that underpin them. Together these processes and principles provide the building blocks for a structured and therefore effective programme management environment.

The programme lifecycle processes and principles ensure that:

- Outcomes for high-level policies and strategies are identified and managed through to successful delivery

- Links are made between the top-level strategic direction of organisations and the management activities required to achieve strategic objectives

- Management focuses attention clearly on the delivery of outcomes and realisation of benefits that are defined and understood at the outset and achieved throughout the lifetime of the programme and beyond

- The goals of a programme remain valid in response to changes outside the programme

- All stakeholders are informed and involved and their interests are appropriately considered

- Senior managers are able to plan and control activities, set priorities and allocate resources for implementation of groups of related projects

- The impact of changes on the organisations and stakeholders involved is managed and the intended change is achieved in the optimum way

- The effective delegation and management of work is executed through discrete projects and related activities

- All issues are recognised and managed to increase the chances for success

- Risks to the programme's successful completion are identified, monitored, managed and controlled in a way acceptable to management

The programme lifecycle processes and principles also increase the probability that change will be delivered under visible control, and the probability of realisation of desired benefits.

4.3 Lifecycle

MSP defines six processes for the effective management of a programme.

Figure 4.2 shows the broad relationship between the six processes within MSP.

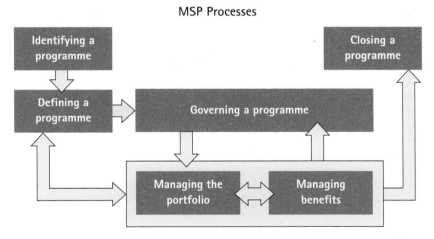

Figure 4.2 MSP processes

Each of the processes is now described, with references to the programme principles where appropriate. Particular attention is paid to those with specific interest for senior management.

4.3.1 Identifying a programme

There are many drivers for change acting on an organisation, from external pressures such as competition, legislation and the wider economic environment, to internal pressures such as new working arrangements resulting from mergers or acquisitions. Organisations respond to these drivers by developing strategies, initiative or polices. These provide the context for change.

The strategy, initiative or policy that is driving the change process generates the Programme Mandate – the trigger for initiating the overall Programme Management process. The Programme Mandate acts as a point of reference for 'Identifying a programme', when the Programme Brief is developed. The Programme Brief provides the basis for deciding whether the programme is justified.

The Programme Brief begins to draw together information about the programme's benefits, costs, timescales and risks. This information should enable senior management to identify what the programme is being set up to achieve and make a decision on whether to commit the investment required to define the programme.

'Identifying a programme' is typically a short process, perhaps taking only a few weeks to complete.

4.3.2 Defining a programme

'Defining a programme' is a crucial process for a programme. It is where the detailed definition and planning for the programme is done and provides the basis for deciding whether to proceed with the programme or not.

The Programme Brief is used as the starting point for refining the programme's objectives and targets into the Programme Definition, which defines what the programme is going to do, how it is going to do it, who is involved, and the Business Case for the programme. The governance framework for the programme is developed, which defines the strategies for quality, stakeholders, issues, risks, benefits, resources and planning and control. The plans are developed providing information on the resources, dependencies and timescales for delivery and realisation of benefits.

Figure 4.3 shows the information documented during this process.

Formal approval is required from senior management to proceed with the programme subject to there being clear evidence that the programme presents a sound basis for the investment.

4.3.3 Governing a programme

The purpose of 'Governing a programme' is to establish and implement the governance arrangements for the programme, which will have been designed during 'Defining a programme'. Governance consists of the functions, processes and procedures that define how the programme is set up, managed and controlled.

Programmes involve a substantial amount of change for individuals, staff, operations, support services and the business environment in which the organisation(s) is operating. Governance

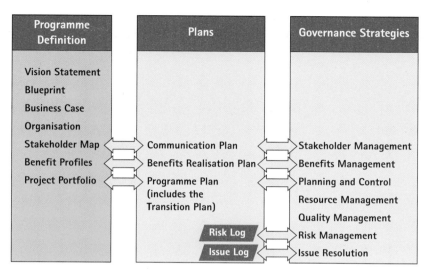

Figure 4.3 Programme information

arrangements need to be established to provide a framework for this upheaval and transformation. Programme governance provides the 'backdrop' for all the activities of directing and managing the programme and achieving the programme's desired outcomes.

The main activities that form part of this process, once the governance arrangements have been put in place, include:

- Reporting, monitoring and control, to include regular progress reporting from the project level to inform the formal progress monitoring at programme level, and the escalation of issues where management intervention is required to keep the programme on track

- Undertaking end-of-tranche reviews of the programme's Business Case, benefits and benefits management process

- Programme communications to ensure that the stakeholders are kept informed and engage in the work of the programme

- Maintaining business as usual during the change process until transition and handover is complete.

4.3.4 Managing the portfolio

'Managing the portfolio' covers the activities for coordinating and managing project delivery according to the Programme Plan. Delivery from the Project Portfolio provides the new capabilities described in the Blueprint. The activities of 'Managing the portfolio' are repeated for each tranche of the programme.

In this sense 'portfolio' means the portfolio of projects within a specific programme (NB: the word 'portfolio' is also in common usage, outside of MSP, to mean the overall portfolio of programmes and projects that an organisation may be investing in at any moment in time).

The main activities that form this process are:

- Project start-up, i.e. commissioning the projects within the Programme Portfolio by ensuring that appropriate individuals are appointed to the project management team and that this team fully understands the Project Brief
- Maintaining the alignment of projects to benefit realisation and programme objectives
- Monitoring progress of individual projects and managing any risks and resolving any issues that impact the programme
- Project closure to ensure that there is a formal handover and transition of outputs into business operation.

4.3.5 Managing benefits

The purpose of 'managing benefits' is to track the benefits from their initial identification to their successful realisation. The activities cover monitoring the progress of the projects to ensure the outputs are fit for purpose and can be integrated into business operations such that the benefits can be realised.

'Managing benefits' also involves the planning and management of the transition from old to new ways of working while ensuring that day-to-day business is maintained. The activities of this process are repeated as necessary for each tranche of the programme.

The main activities that form this process are:

- Establishing benefits measurements, in particular ensuring that the 'before' state is measured so that an assessment can be made as to whether the 'after' measurements indicate an improvement or not
- Benefits monitoring and measurement
- Transition management, i.e. preparing the business operations for the implementation of the project outputs and then implementing the necessary changes
- Supporting changes to culture and personnel during the transition.

'Managing the portfolio' and 'Managing benefits' are distinct processes, but they need to work closely together to harmonise the programme objectives with project delivery and benefit realisation.

4.3.6 Closing a programme

Programmes tend to last for many months – typically, a few years. There is often a danger of allowing the programme to drift on, as if it is part of normal business. The purpose of 'Closing a programme' is to ensure the focus is on achieving the end goal of the programme, formally recognising when the programme is completed and has delivered the required new capabilities described in the Blueprint. Benefits will have been realised during the running of the programme; however, some benefits, and possibly the majority of them, may not be fully realised until some time after the last project has delivered. 'Closing a programme' identifies the need for future assessment of benefit realisation as well as a formal review of those achieved so far.

The main activities that form this process are:

- Confirming programme closure involving the formal confirmation that the Business Case has been satisfied, all projects have been completed satisfactorily, and any remaining handover or transition activities required have been defined and assigned to relevant business operations
- Programme review to assess the delivery of the complete Blueprint and realisation of the overall benefits and also assess and evaluate the performance of the programme and its management processes.

4.4 Principles

Some of the principles of MSP have been referred to in the above description of the lifecycle processes. For completeness, this section provides a high-level description of each principle.

4.4.1 Organisation and leadership

Establishing the optimum organisation for a programme means defining the roles required, the responsibilities of each of these roles, and the management structures and reporting arrangements needed to deliver the programme's desired outcomes. Leadership, at all levels, is essential. Skilled and experienced individuals with clearly defined authority, accountability and responsibility are vital for leadership to be effective.

Programme Management is most effective when issues are debated freely and risks evaluated openly. This requires a leadership style and culture that encourages the flow of information between projects and the programme level. Every opportunity to advance the programme towards its goals should be welcomed and converted into constructive progress.

The leadership roles identified within the programme organisation structure proposed by MSP reflect the four critical success factors mentioned earlier. These roles are:

Sponsoring Group with Senior Responsible Owner

- The Sponsoring Group represents those senior managers who are responsible for the investment decision. They provide top-level endorsement of the rationale and objectives for the programme, promote and support the changes introduced by the programme, and champion the implementation of the new capabilities delivered by the programme to ensure that the expected benefits are realised and the desired outcomes achieved

- The Senior Responsible Owner owns the **Vision** and has overall accountability for the programme, together with personal responsibility for ensuring that it meets its objectives and realises the expected benefits. The individual who fulfils this role should be a peer member of the Sponsoring Group.

Programme Manager

- The Programme Manager is responsible, on behalf of the Senior Responsible Owner, for successful delivery of the new capability. The role requires the effective **co-ordination of the projects and their interdependencies**, and any risks and other issues that may arise. In most cases, the Programme Manager will typically work full-time on the programme, as the role is crucial for creating and maintaining enthusiasm.

Business Change Manager(s)

- Where substantial change in business operations is required, the individual(s) appointed to the role of Business Change Manager will be responsible for **transition management**, creating the new business structures, operations and working practices.

- The role of Business Change Manager is primarily **benefits-focused**. The Business Change Manager role is responsible, on behalf of the Senior Responsible Owner, for defining the benefits, assessing progress towards realisation, and achieving measured improvements. This need to define and realise benefits in terms of measured improvements in business performance means that the Business Change Manager role must be 'business-side', in order to provide a bridge between the programme and business operations.

4.4.2 Benefits management

The fundamental reason for beginning a programme is to realise benefits through change. The change may be to do things differently, to do different things, or to do things that will influence others to change. Realising benefits requires active management throughout the change process. The identification, monitoring and measurement of benefits is a fundamental part of successful programme management.

The change results in desired outcomes: the things that happen as a result of the changes made. Benefits are the quantification of these outcomes and are used to direct the programme and inform decision-making along the way. Change may also result in other side-effects and consequences, often leading to dis-benefits – negative impacts of change. Side-effects and consequences may also lead to additional, possibly unplanned, benefits. Benefits management covers all these aspects.

4.4.3 Stakeholder management and communications

Over the life of a programme, there will be many individuals or groups with an interest or involvement with it, or who are affected by its activities and outcomes. These are the programme's **stakeholders**. They include those managing and working within the programme and those who are directly or indirectly contributing to, or affected by, the programme or its outcomes.

Understanding stakeholders' interests in the programme, and the impact that the programme will have on them, and then implementing a strategy to address their issues and needs is an essential part of successful programme management.

4.4.4 Risk management and issue resolution

Programmes are established to deliver change through the co-ordinated execution of multiple projects. Programmes typically involve diverse groups of stakeholders, together with contributions from service providers, suppliers and other third-party organisations. This, together with the inevitable upheaval caused by change, makes the programme environment uncertain, complex and dynamic. At any point during a programme, there will be events or situations that may adversely affect the direction of the programme, the delivery of its outputs, realisation of expected benefits or the achievement of desired outcomes. These events or situations are the risks and issues that the programme has to manage and resolve.

Risks are things that may happen at some point in the future and require positive management to reduce their likelihood of happening, their impact on the programme, or both. Issues are things happening now that are affecting the programme in some way and need to be actively dealt with and resolved. Risks, should they occur, become issues. The task of risk management is to keep the programme's exposure to risk at an acceptable level.

Issues can arise at any time during the programme, and will require specific and usually immediate management action. The task of issue resolution is to prevent the issue from threatening the programme's chances of achieving a successful outcome.

4.4.5 Programme planning and control

Programme planning and control is not simply project planning and control on a larger scale, rather it is a combination of various planning and monitoring considerations. All these aspects have a part to play and are set out and brought together in the Programme Plan, a key control document for the programme. The elements that contribute to programme planning, and the central Programme Plan include The Vision Statement, Blueprint, Benefits, Projects, Resources, Stakeholder needs, Risks and assumptions, Timetable, Progress monitoring and Transition.

Programme planning is a continual activity throughout a programme. At the beginning of a programme, it involves determining and defining **what** needs to be done and **when**, how long things should take, **who** will do them, **how** will things be monitored, **who** needs to be involved, and **what** risks may affect progress. Developing and maintaining the Programme Plan requires the ongoing co-ordination of all the project plans. The focus for programme planning is on the interdependencies between the projects and any dependencies on external factors outside the control of the programme.

4.4.6 Business Case management

The Business Case is an aggregation of specific information about the programme: benefits and the risks to achieving them, costs and timescales. The Business Case presents the optimum 'mix' of this information that can be used to judge whether or not the programme is (and remains) desirable, viable and achievable. The Business Case effectively describes what the *value* is to the sponsoring organisation from the outcomes of the programme. Managing the Business Case is about *value management* of benefits, costs, timescales and risks.

4.4.7 Quality management

Quality, as applied to a programme, embraces many different aspects, including:

- The quality of the programme's leadership and management processes, including the information needed to make decisions and the reliability of the information provided
- The quality of its deliverables, meaning their 'fitness for purpose'
- The quality of its assessment and measurement activities.

Quality management is a continuous process throughout the life of a programme.

Summary

In summary, the key features and resulting benefits from MSP are that:

- MSP works because it addresses the four critical success factors for effective programme management; namely, having in place:
  - A clear and consistent **Vision** of the changed business or other outcome
  - Co-ordination of a number of **projects and their interdependencies**
  - Leadership, influence, management and direction of the **transition**, including handling cultural change
  - A focus on **benefits** and the internal and external threats to their achievement
- MSP ensures that only programmes that address these factors, as reflected within the Business Case, are undertaken
- MSP maintains focus on the end-goal of a programme through two complementary documents: the Vision Statement and the Blueprint. These provide a guiding light to the programme amongst the complexity, uncertainty, change and risk accompanying unbounded change
- MSP recognises that major change and the attendant benefits are more likely to be achieved through a phased approach, and hence the programme is divided into a number of tranches. Each tranche delivers a step change in capability and enables the organisation to realise benefits progressively during the life of the programme
- MSP guides the programme through its lifecycle by identifying six high-level processes that describe the necessary activities and outputs required for the management of the programme
- MSP outlines a number of key principles which an organisation can adapt and adopt to meet its own particular circumstances
- MSP works because it ensures clear roles and responsibilities for the sponsorship and direction of the programme and for the management of the portfolio of projects, the transition to new ways of working and the realisation of the benefits.

5
PRINCE2

Chapter 3 summarised the role of programmes and projects in translating strategy into meaningful actions. This included an overview of PRINCE2 as a proven project management approach. This chapter identifies how PRINCE2 facilitates the delivery of projects within controlled environments and describes the benefits. PRINCE2 applies equally whether the project is part of a programme or is a stand-alone project.

5.1   Overview

PRINCE2's key philosophy is that its Business Case must drive the project. The Business Case documents the justification for undertaking a project based on the estimated cost of development and implementation against the risks and the anticipated business benefits. If a satisfactory Business Case does not exist at the start of a project, the project should not be started. Likewise, if the justification disappears during the course of the project, the project should be stopped.

The business benefits are realised as a result of the organisation using the deliverables from the project. Accordingly, another key principle of PRINCE2 is its focus on deliverables, or products rather than activity. This creates a better environment in which to control a project's likely outcome. Product or deliverable-based planning is a well established project management technique. The products are clearly defined at the outset and the dependencies between them are mapped, allowing the project to remain focused on achieving business results, whatever the current activity.

PRINCE2 is defined in terms of a customer/supplier environment. This assumes that there will be a customer who will specify the desired product, make use of the final product and probably pay for the project, and a supplier who will provide the resources and skills to create that product. This environment is reflected in the PRINCE2 project management team structure.

Clear roles and responsibilities are key if the project processes are to be executed effectively. PRINCE2 provides a model of the organisational requirements that includes the roles and responsibilities of senior management. In PRINCE2, senior management controls the project through the Project Board which owns the project and is responsible for delivery of benefits and controlling costs. Since the Project Board reflects the customer/supplier stakeholders, any decisions or changes to the baselined plan in terms of costs, time or specification are endorsed by it, scope for the unexpected is minimised and all parties remain 'onside' with each decision.

The checks, balances and results focus of PRINCE2 contributes to the control necessary to accommodate the inevitable changes to the original plan without invalidating the purpose or scope of the project. PRINCE2 recognises that changes to the original plan will occur and provides processes for dealing with these changes. Change, whether voluntary or involuntary, can have a huge impact on the success of a project and needs to be carefully monitored and managed to ensure the scope and output remain appropriate to the Business Case: changes that are missed or ignored can have a catastrophic impact. PRINCE2 deals with the unexpected by ensuring that:

- Procedures are in place for issues to be surfaced early and closed appropriately
- The Business Case for the project and the specification of changes required are baselined and that changes to the original Business Case are only approved if the appropriate control processes are followed.

The method provides a phased approach to the project and allows for a number of review points. These review points, usually after each stage of the project, allow for the original justification for the project to be scrutinised and reaffirmed or adjusted as circumstances dictate. The key benefit for senior management is that the project needs to clear these control hurdles if it is to continue to the next stage. A project unable to justify the move to the next stage may be closed. Senior management therefore have control to direct the project and are well positioned to ensure that the planned benefits (original or adjusted) continue to justify the project.

Poor risk management is an area of historic weakness in change projects. PRINCE2 provides processes for risk identification, analysis and mitigation planning. The approach ensures that risks are visible throughout the life of the project, and that any change in the status of these risks is understood early enough to allow sufficient time for management to assess the potential implications and initiate appropriate countermeasures.

5.2   Processes and components

PRINCE2 is constructed around a process-based approach to project management. The processes clearly define the management activities to be carried out during the life of the project. The intensity with which each of these processes is undertaken can be varied according to project circumstances or particular organisational needs. However, the principle is that if each process is applied properly the scope for loss of control, unexpected deviation from the objectives, and surprises, is minimised.

Additionally, a number of project management components, which are applied at appropriate points in the processes, are also described.

Figure 5.1 shows the major project management processes and the components that underpin them. Together these processes and components provide the building blocks for a controlled and therefore effective project management environment.

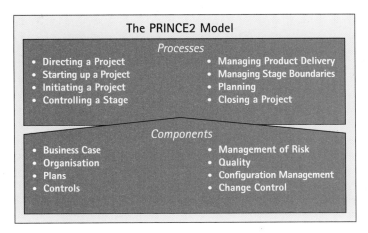

Figure 5.1 PRINCE2 processes and components

The project processes and components ensure that:

- The goals of a project can be reviewed and adjusted in light of experience

- There is a 'big picture' to support Executive decisions regarding resource allocation and reallocation

- The impact of changes can be assessed and decisions in response to these changes ensure that the organisation's resources remain optimised and targeted at the desired benefits

- Activity can be organised allowing for effective delegation of management

- Risks are continually identified and assessed allowing for effective mitigation strategies for each to be developed and tracked

- Issues surface early and are therefore more likely to be managed optimally

- Communication to all stakeholders is timely, accurate and targeted at the appropriate audience

- The benefits are understood and are kept visible for the duration

- The critical path through a complex set of activities and deliverables can be described simply, tracked and adjusted as dictated by changes in the original drivers of the project.

5.3   The processes

PRINCE2 defines eight processes for the effective management of a project.

Figure 5.2 shows the broad relationship between the eight processes within PRINCE2.

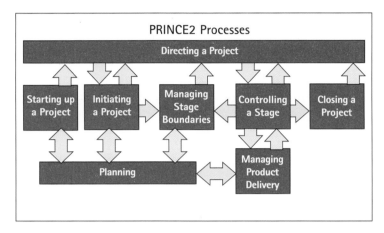

Figure 5.2 PRINCE2 processes

The diagram is a simplified view of the process model, as individual organisations will want to tailor it to meet their specific requirements. However, every project will need to apply each of the processes to some extent, to be determined at the initiation stage.

Each of the processes is now described, with references to the project components where appropriate. Particular attention is paid to those with specific interest for senior management.

5.3.1 Directing a Project

This process provides the senior management responsible for the project with the means to direct the project's resources. *Directing a Project* is effectively a decision-making process. A key principle of PRINCE2 is that senior management should be able to manage the project on an exception basis. This reduces the time that senior management need to commit to the project, but there is not the loss of control that is sometimes seen as a benefit of using a more hands-on approach.

The process covers the whole duration of the project from start-up to closure and has five major activities:

1   Authorising the initiation of the project

2   Approval for the project to commence

3   Checking that the project is still justifiable at key interim review points

4   Monitoring progress and providing ad hoc direction

5   Ensuring that the project comes to a controlled close and that lessons and experiences are learned for the benefit of future projects.

5.3.2 Starting up a Project

This is generally a short process when compared with the duration of the project and it has four primary objectives:

1   Clarifying and communicating the aims and benefits of the project in the form of a Project Brief

2   Designing and appointing the project management team

3   Deciding on the Project Approach, i.e. how the project will deliver the required solution

4   Planning the work needed to draw up the 'contract' between the Project Board and Project Manager.

The outputs from this process should enable the Project Board to answer the basic question: 'Do we have a viable and worthwhile project?'.

5.3.3 Initiating a Project

Initiating a Project draws up a 'contract' in the form of a Project Initiation Document (PID) between the Project Board and the Project Manager. This document is baselined and any changes to the project have to be assessed against it to determine whether the project is still justified. The PID is also the control mechanism that allows the project's progress to be monitored. Ultimately the project's success will be measured against the original objectives of time, cost and quality as defined in the PID.

The PID would normally include the following:

Background

This gives the main events that led to the need for the project.

The Project Definition

The Project Board must satisfy itself that the project objectives are still achievable. The remainder of this section would be a refinement of the Project Brief and Project Approach.

Project Approach

This indicates what method will be used to provide a solution to the Project's objectives.

Controls

The Project Initiation Document will include details of the controls that will enable the Project Board to keep overall control of the project. This will include step-by-step approval for the project to proceed via a series of end stage assessments, confirmation of the tolerance level for the project, and details of what will happen if any stage exceeds its agreed tolerance. There should be information on the frequency and content of reports from the Project Manager to the Project Board, together with details of how the Project Manager intends to control the project on a day-to-day basis. The Project Board must satisfy itself that these controls are adequate for the nature of the project.

Business Case

The Project Board has to confirm that an adequate and suitable Business Case exists for the project and that it shows a viable project. Information on the expected benefits and savings should be supplied and approved by the customer. The project costs should come from the Project Plan.

Project Plan

The Project Plan gives an overall view of the major products, timescale and cost for the project. Any wide variation between this and any previous forecast for the project should be examined and the Project Board should assure itself of the continued validity and achievability of the plan and reasons for the variation. The Project Plan needs to be co-ordinated with any relevant strategic and programme management plans.

Risk Log

The project management team should identify any risks facing the project's products. The Project Board should ensure that risks are being tracked and mitigated as effectively as possible.

Project organisation

Most, if not all, of the appointments of the project management team will have been finalised during *Starting up a Project*. These now have to be formally confirmed and any late appointments negotiated. Each member of the team should have agreed their role and this agreement is one of the items that the Project Board has to confirm.

Communication Plan

This should reflect the information needs and timing of communications between the Project Manager, the Project Board and any other interested parties. It includes communication in both directions between the parties. The Communication Plan will contain details of any required co-operation from outside the project, plus links to corporate or programme management. It is the responsibility of the Project Board to obtain this and confirm the availability.

Project Quality Plan

The Project Quality Plan must state how the project intends to meet the customer's quality expectations and where quality responsibilities have been allocated. The Project Board must satisfy itself that the quality expectations have been correctly translated from the Project Brief and that the Project Quality Plan will deliver them.

A careful and considered project initiation is crucial to a successful project because the costs of the project are described and committed at this stage. Many projects fail due to a poorly executed project initiation stage so senior management have to be confident that the Business Case is a true reflection of the likely project costs and benefits. Figure 5.3 shows the relationship between project phases and the extent to which costs are committed at any given point.

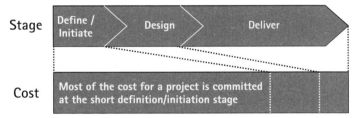

Figure 5.3 Most of the cost is committed during the relatively short project definition/initiation stage

Organisations should resist the temptation to move from definition to design too quickly. All too often there is pressure to move from initiation or definition to design driven by the erroneous belief that this will demonstrate that a project is making progress. The problem that this approach presents is that the design can be based on fundamentally flawed understanding of the real costs of delivering the planned business benefits.

To illustrate this, Figure 5.4 shows the relative costs associated with correcting errors at a range of points in the project lifecycle. It highlights very clearly the imperative for a robust initiation and design as the cost of correcting an error identified in live running is 100 times the cost of correcting an error identified in the definition phase.

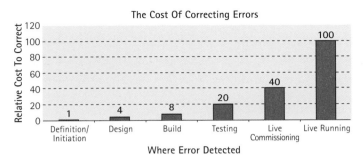

Figure 5.4 The cost of quality

The following example of a recent project, window on practice 5.1, highlights the problems associated when a poor design has resulted from an unclear initiation process.

Window on practice 5.1

A major UK bank developed a new capability based on a flawed Business Case. As the objectives of the **project** were unclear from the outset the **project** ran massively over budget in terms of time and cost and the **deliverable** was regarded as being very poor **quality**.

The bank is now constrained by a poor design and cannot implement its business plan for the new capability.

PRINCE2's rigorous requirements in the earliest stages of a project minimise scope for starting work with incomplete information or justification.

5.3.4 Controlling a Stage

PRINCE2's *Controlling a Stage* process describes the monitoring and control activities required to keep a stage on track by providing the information required to allow the anticipation of, and response to, any changes to the business specification or to the status of the project risks.

This is a core process for the Project Manager and makes up the bulk of the day-to-day control of the work that is being conducted. Throughout a stage, this will consist of a cycle of:

- Authorising work to be done
- Monitoring progress information about that work
- Watching for and assessing Project Issues
- Reviewing the situation and triggering new Work Packages

- Reporting
- Taking any necessary corrective action.

If changes are observed that are forecast to cause deviations beyond agreed tolerances, this process also covers the activities of bringing the situation to the attention of the Project Board.

5.3.5 Managing Product Delivery

Managing Product Delivery produces a contract between the project and the specialists who will produce deliverables. This contract is particularly important where work is being outsourced to a third-party supplier. PRINCE2 calls the work agreed in this process a 'Work Package'. It covers details about schedules, quality and reporting requirements. The primary benefit of this approach is that it removes the chances of there being any ambiguity between parties as to what is required by whom and by when. This clarity is possible as all partners in the project are using the common language of PRINCE2.

5.3.6 Managing Stage Boundaries

As described earlier, the project is more manageable and provides greater control for senior management if it is broken down into stages. The key business benefit of this is that senior management can decide if the project is still justified at a number of points in the project lifecycle. *Managing Stage Boundaries* facilitates:

- Planning the next stage of the project
- Updating of the Project Plan
- Updating of the Business Case
- Updating of the risk assessment
- Reporting on the outcome and performance of the stage just completed
- Seeking approval from senior management to move into the next stage.

The above information is drawn together by the Project Manager and then presented to the Project Board at an End Stage Assessment.

5.3.7 Planning

Planning is an ongoing process throughout the project. To avoid wasted time and effort PRINCE2 stipulates that detailed planning is only carried out for the next stage to be undertaken. This allows the experience of the current and preceding stages to inform the planning of the next stage. This type of planning process supports PRINCE2's product-based approach. The planning process aims to:

- Define and analyse the plan's products or outcomes
- Identify the necessary activities to produce the products or outcomes
- Identify the dependencies between the products and the activities needed to produce them
- Schedule the resources
- Analyse the risks
- Describe the planning assumptions and quality steps.

Planning must be pragmatic and constructed to provide both a summary of the project to senior management and a more detailed view to allow the Project Manager to manage resources at a more local level. Typically, Project Managers will require a level of plan that allows them to manage activity on a weekly basis. PRINCE2 encourages pragmatic planning and thus avoids the trap that many organisations fall into of planning in too much detail too far into the future. Window on practice 5.2 illustrates the problems of poor planning.

Window on practice 5.2

An insurance company entered into a partnership with a major software provider. The objective for the project was highly ambitious and early estimates indicated that the project would use several hundred staff for a two-year period. The third party had limited knowledge of the business but was allowed to manage the project. The chief project planner undertook to produce the plan and was soon floundering in too much detail. The initial plan presented to senior management took three months to produce. It was bound in a folder two inches thick. There was no summary available. The plan was so complex it was estimated that it would take three weeks to produce a weekly summary.

Six months into the project there was still no credible plan available. The company decided that the planning fiasco was a clear indication that the provider had inadequate control of the project and the contract was terminated.

5.3.8 Closing a Project

The purpose of this process is to execute a controlled close to the project. The process covers the Project Manager's work to wrap up the project either at its end or at a premature close. Most of the work is to prepare input to the Project Board to obtain its confirmation that the project may close.

The main objectives of *Closing a Project* are to:

- Check the extent to which the objectives or aims set out in the Project Initiation Document have been met

- Confirm the customer's satisfaction with products and benefits
- Confirm that maintenance and operation arrangements are in place
- Make any recommendations for future work
- Capture lessons resulting from the project and ensure these are communicated to improve processes for future projects.

5.4   The components

Some of the components of PRINCE2 have been referred to in the above description of the project processes. For completeness, this section provides a high-level description of each component.

5.4.1 Business Case

As mentioned at the beginning of this chapter, PRINCE2's key philosophy is that its Business Case must drive the project. In PRINCE2 the Business Case is supported by other documents (such as the Risk Log) that form the Project Initiation Document. Accordingly, as a minimum the Business Case should contain the following information:

- **Reasons**. An explanation of why the project is needed
- **Options**. An outline description of the various options that have been considered
- **Benefits expected**. A description of each benefit in measurable terms
- **Risks**. A summary of the key risks facing the project
- **Costs and timescale**. The estimated costs and timescales for the project
- **Investment appraisal**. A balance between the development, operational, maintenance and support costs against the financial value of the benefits over a period of time.

5.4.2 Organisation

As already outlined, PRINCE2's Project Board is the organisation of the senior management and group responsible for the project, including the sponsor, the senior business owner responsible for the delivery of the benefits and a senior representative of a supplier organisation. As such it is the principal forum for directing a project, effectively the decision-making body charged with all approvals of changes to the original Business Case. The exact design of the Project Board should fit with the organisation's reporting framework.

PRINCE2 provides for a single focus for the day-to-day management of the project in the form of the Project Manager.

In the design of the rest of the project management team consideration should be given to providing:

- Project Assurance roles to support the Project Board
- Team Managers and Project Support to support the Project Manager

5.4.3 Plans

The PRINCE2 planning structure allows for a plan to be broken down into lower-level plans containing more detail. PRINCE2 proposes three levels of plan:

- **Project Plan**. An overview of the total project, used by the Project Board as a basis against which to monitor actual costs and project progress stage by stage
- **Stage Plans**. Produced towards the end of the previous stage, this is the basis for the Project Manager's day-to-day control
- **Team Plans**. These are optional depending on the size and complexity of the project.

5.4.4 Controls

A key control for the Project Board in terms of enabling them to manage by exception is tolerance. This is the permissible deviation from the stage plan without bringing the deviation to the attention of the Project Board. The two standard elements of tolerance are time and cost. However tolerances can also be defined for scope, risk, benefit and quality.

Another key principle for controlling a project is to break the whole into a number of manageable stages. These stages afford a number of important control points for the senior management team to review the ongoing justification for the project and decide whether it should be allowed to proceed into the next stage. This approach is of particular benefit where a project has a lengthy duration. In addition, subdivision can help motivate the team as the review points allow them to see the progress made at the end of each stage and their efforts can be recognised at these stages. This phasing also encourages the early release of benefits; it avoids having all benefits planned for delivery at the end of a project and therefore prone to accumulated risk and delay.

5.4.5 Management of risk

Risk is of particular interest to senior management and calls for careful consideration throughout the project lifecycle.

PRINCE2 describes a risk management cycle consisting of:

- Risk analysis
  - Identify the risks
  - Evaluate the risks
  - Identify suitable responses to risk
  - Select risk actions
- Risk management
  - Plan and resource
  - Monitor and report.

Risks are identified at the outset of the project and can be viewed from two main perspectives – probability and impact. Probability is the evaluated likelihood of a particular outcome actually happening. Risk impact is the evaluated effect or result of a particular outcome actually happening (becoming an issue). Another aspect that could be considered is proximity, i.e. a prediction which reflects the timing of the risk.

Suitable responses to risk break down into broadly five types:

- Prevention
- Reduction
- Transference
- Acceptance
- Contingency.

To maintain the visibility of risks they are captured and maintained in a risk log. This log is a key component of the project reporting process to the senior team.

One of the success factors for effective risk management is the assignment of each risk to a clear owner whose responsibility it is to monitor the risk and who has the authority to make decisions to bring the risk to a resolution in the shortest possible time. Readers may like to refer to OGC's *Management of Risk: Guidance for Practitioners* (The Stationery Office Ltd, 2004) for details of best practice in risk management.

5.4.6 Quality

PRINCE2 builds quality work into a project from the very outset and provides key events to assess throughout the project whether it is being achieved. Achieving the required quality of product (and the right quality of project management) is an essential feature of any project. Far too often a check on the quality of the final product(s) is left until one of the final steps of a project – with the resulting delays and expense until any failings are put right. This assumes that any quality flaws were not built into the product at specification or design time. Discovery of such quality flaws near the end of a project can be impossible to correct fully.

5.4.7   Change Control and Configuration Management

No project can be considered under control if it allows uncontrolled changes to what it was agreed that the project would deliver. Such changes can destroy cost, time, scope and quality control. PRINCE2's components include both Change Control and Configuration Management; protection and security for the project's products. The activities necessary for the effective working of these components are included seamlessly in the PRINCE2 processes.

Summary

In summary, the key features and resulting benefits from PRINCE2 are that:

- PRINCE2 works because it ensures through the development of a Business Case that the right projects are undertaken based on a clearly supportable justification

- PRINCE2's delivery-focused approach describes products which are essential for the realisation of the benefits the project enables

- PRINCE2 breaks the project into manageable stages. At the end of each stage the justification for the project can be reviewed and reaffirmed

- PRINCE2 adopts a pragmatic approach to the management of project risks and changes to the baselined specification

- PRINCE2 provides a process-based approach to project management, describing the management activities that need to be carried out during the project lifecycle

- PRINCE2 outlines a number of project management components which are applied at appropriate points in the processes

- PRINCE2 works because it ensures clear roles and responsibilities. Ownership of the definition and realisation of the benefits is clear from the outset. Senior management perform the role of high-level decision-maker, accommodated through the Project Board.

6

MANAGING PROGRAMMES AND PROJECTS – KEY LESSONS ADDRESSED BY MSP AND PRINCE2

This book has advocated the need for a controlled environment for the successful management of change. This conclusion has been drawn from extensive research and actual examples from both the public and private sectors. This chapter summarises the key lessons drawn from that research and indicates how MSP and PRINCE2 can help organisations achieve successful and sustainable change.

One way of summarising the key lessons learned is to consider the common causes of programme and project failure. Research suggests that the most common causes are as follows:

- Lack of clear links between the programme or project and the organisation's key strategic priorities, including agreed measures of success

- Lack of clear senior management ownership and leadership

- Lack of effective engagement with stakeholders

- Lack of skills and proven approach to programme/project management and risk management

- Too little attention to breaking development and implementation into manageable steps

- Evaluation of proposals driven by initial price rather than long-term value for money (especially securing delivery of business benefits)

- Lack of understanding of, and contact with, the supply industry at senior levels in the organisation

- Lack of effective project team integration between clients, the supplier team and the supply chain.

This section demonstrates how MSP and PRINCE2 can help organisations avoid these causes.

6.1 Links to key strategic priorities

Both MSP and PRINCE2 encourage organisations to recognise the link between strategic objectives and the objectives of individual programmes and projects.

Within MSP this link is established initially through the Programme Mandate which is provided by the Sponsoring Group, and this is then confirmed within the Programme Brief which is approved by the Programme Senior Responsible Owner. During programme definition a fuller understanding of the link to strategic objectives is established through the creation of the programme's:

- Vision Statement (an outward-facing description of the new capabilities resulting from programme delivery)

- Blueprint (a model of the business organisation, its working practices and processes, the information it requires and the technology that will be needed to deliver the capability described in the Vision Statement)

- Business Case (captures the strategic objectives for the programme, reflecting the Vision Statement, and alignment with the organisational context and business environment).

Similarly within PRINCE2, the link is established initially through the Project Mandate provided by corporate or programme management; this is confirmed within the Project Brief which is approved by the Project Board. During project initiation the project Business Case is developed which describes the reasons and full justification for undertaking the project; these should support the organisation's strategic objectives.

6.2 Senior management ownership and leadership

Co-ordinating all the aspects of change requires effective leadership and that is only possible where the responsibility for programmes and projects falls to a senior member of the management team. If responsibility is not clear at the outset, then it is almost impossible for a programme or project to succeed.

Both MSP and PRINCE2 provide for the establishment of roles and responsibilities that enable and encourage senior management to be actively involved in the ownership and leadership of programmes and projects.

MSP establishes a Sponsoring Group which represents those senior managers who are responsible for the investment decision, defining the direction of the business and establishing frameworks to achieve the desired objectives. From this group is appointed the Senior Responsible Owner who has overall accountability for the programme, together with personal responsibility for ensuring that it meets its objectives and realises the expected benefits.

Within PRINCE2 there is the Project Board which represents at managerial level the business, user and supplier interests of the project. The Project Board are responsible for making decisions and for the commitment of resources to the project.

6.3 Engagement with stakeholders

Stakeholder management and communications is one of the key principles within MSP. Understanding stakeholders' interests in the programme, and the impact that the programme will have on them, and then implementing a strategy to address their issues and needs, is an essential part of successful programme management. MSP encourages proactive stakeholder management through the production of a Stakeholder Management Strategy (which includes a Stakeholder Map, an analysis of influence and impact of each stakeholder group and describes how the programme will engage with them) and a Communication Plan (which describes the key communication messages and the responsibilities, channels and schedule of communications).

PRINCE2 does not provide the same level of focus on stakeholder management but it does cover the creation of a Communication Plan which identifies interested parties, the information required by these stakeholders and the frequency, method and format of communication.

6.4 Proven approach to Programme and Project Management

To achieve a radical step-change in business performance an organisation needs to develop an integrated and controlled approach to the definition and delivery of its corporate aspirations. This book has described the solution as a Programme and Project Management Environment, which gathers into a single framework all the required elements that collectively provide the conditions needed to drive organisational success. We have discussed the need for a cultural revolution where the solution to managing business changes is not to simply purchase a 'solution' and hope that it succeeds. There is a real need for the top team to champion the Programme and Project Management Environment and lead the organisation on a journey that many may find quite alien from existing practices. The key lesson for senior management is that they must grasp control of the current environment and, through skilful and enthusiastic leadership, implement the Programme and Project Management Environment in such a way that others willingly follow. Each organisation will need to decide for itself how best to implement this new capability; however, MSP and PRINCE2 can provide the fast track to dramatic increases in business performance through its boldness of attack and a radical approach to implementation.

6.4.1 Improved programme and project management skills

Good leaders who have a clear responsibility for change are not sufficient by themselves. Good management needs to permeate the whole organisation. The leader will need a team that is able to deliver. The delivery of change is a challenging task and highly skilled and experienced programme and project workers are vital to success.

The MSP and PRINCE2 management processes allow for a repeatable application of these skills. As a common language is used, the resources can be moved from programme to programme and from project to project and the knowledge and experience from each is developed and grown to become a key company asset. The increase in capability for the organisation can be measured through the formal examination and accreditation of staff within MSP's and PRINCE2's training and professional development structure.

6.4.2 Greater focus on risks

Focusing on the delivery of business benefits requires a greater awareness of the potential risks to the organisation of programme and/or project failure. There are specific actions within programme and project management that need to be taken in the area of risk management.

Within both MSP and PRINCE2 risk management is defined as a key management process. Programme and project risks are identified at the outset and actively tracked and managed for the duration of the programme or project. Risks are rated in terms of their probability and impact and recorded on a formal Risk Log. Each risk is assigned an owner who is responsible for monitoring the risk and the implementation of mitigating plans to address them. The risks and the status of the actions to contain them are made visible at a senior management level by the Risk Log being an integral part of the reporting process.

However, risk is not only present within programmes and projects. Risks appear at all levels within an organisation where there are objectives to be achieved and decisions to be made; i.e. at the strategic, programme, project and operational levels. Just as organisations would benefit from adopting common approaches to managing their programmes and projects, there are similar benefits to be realised from adopting a common approach to the management of risk. Such an approach is provided by the OGC best practice guide *Management of Risk: Guidance for Practitioners* (M_o_R).

Risks associated with:

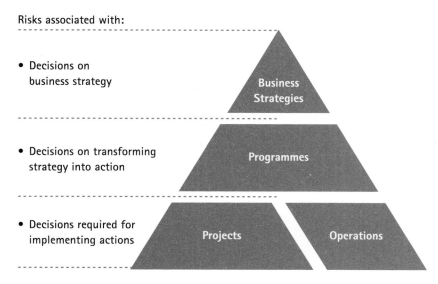

- Decisions on business strategy

- Decisions on transforming strategy into action

- Decisions required for implementing actions

Figure 6.1 Risks across all organisational levels

6.5   Manageable steps

Managing the risk of programme or project failure can be made easier if ambitious and complex programmes and projects are broken up into manageable phases. This phasing will also help to keep the team motivated as they can see the progress being made. This approach also avoids the risks associated with one big delivery at the end of the programme or project.

MSP organises the projects within a programme into groups structured around distinct step-changes in capability and benefit delivery. These groups are known as 'tranches'. The programme's Business Case, benefits and benefits management process are reviewed at the end of each tranche.

At the heart of PRINCE2 is a stage-by-stage approach to planning and control which allows for the project's initial justification to be reviewed at various key points. The staged approach also allows for pragmatic planning where only the next stage of a project is planned in detail, resulting in less wasted time on detailed planning at the outset and replanning along the way.

6.6   Evaluation of value for money

Central to both MSP and PRINCE2 is the concept of a Business Case, used to justify the investment in the programme or project. In both instances the Business Case draws together information relating to the:

- Reasons (for undertaking the change)
- Options (describing the different options considered in terms of how the programmes outcomes or project outputs could be achieved)
- Benefits (expressed in measurable terms)
- Risks (facing the successful delivery of the programme or project's benefits)
- Costs and timescales (covering the whole-life costs and timeframe)
- Investment appraisal (based on the above information).

Also covered by both MSP and PRINCE2 is the need to review the programme or project Business Case at regular interval, at least at the end of each tranche or stage.

6.7 Improved supplier relationships

Often, the change agenda cannot be delivered by the organisation alone. Suppliers have a major role to play, and implementing an improved approach to managing change will be impossible if relationships with suppliers or procurement are poor.

The focus within MSP is on the management of those supplier resources that are shared across more than one of the projects within the portfolio. MSP also recognises that procurement is a common aspect within programmes and will require access to procurement expertise to carry out or advise on procurement activities.

A Programme Board may be used to bring together key stakeholders (such as major suppliers), partners or investors as part of the programme's organisation structure.

PRINCE2 has the concept of a customer–supplier relationship at its very core. Through this attitude the project can draw up formal contracts for the work that a supplier will undertake and the deliverables to be provided. When the supplier organisation also adopts PRINCE2 this enables effective cross-company working with both organisations using the same language.

The Project Board ensures that key stakeholders, including third-party suppliers, are appropriately involved in the decision-making process.

6.8 Why do MSP and PRINCE2 work?

There are several fundamental reasons why MSP and PRINCE2 work in almost all instances:

- Because MSP and PRINCE2 are so widely used and have been developed from and into best practice, an organisation can adopt them and avoid the drawbacks associated with ad hoc approaches

- By using a consistent and repeatable set of processes the organisation can build up a valuable asset bank of programme and project experiences

- Resources can be moved freely between programmes and projects, thanks to the common language MSP and PRINCE2 bring to all programmes and projects

- The controlled start, progress and close allow the organisation to focus on the benefits it wants to achieve rather than unduly worrying over how it will deliver them

- The principle of management by exception means that this control does not come with an excessive cost in valuable senior management time

- Management by exception allows senior management to delegate with confidence, allowing them to become involved at a detailed level only when the parameters are breached or when a high-level decision on programme or project direction is required.

Summary

Research and experience demonstrate that an organisation will greatly improve its chances of successfully managing change when it adopts proven, structured and controlled approaches to programme and project management such as MSP and PRINCE2.

MSP and PRINCE2 can offer organisations access to a fast track to the skills and set-up that will enable them to manage change well and deliver business benefits through programme and project management.

GLOSSARY

Note: This glossary combines those provided with the MSP and the PRINCE2 best practice guides.

Where a term refers to a management role or management information/product used within one of these guides a reference to the guide is included in brackets.

Where both guides include a term (or similar term) but with a different description, both descriptions are provided.

Acceptance Criteria (PRINCE2)
A prioritised list of criteria that the final product(s) must meet before the customer will accept them; a measurable definition of what must be done for the final product to be acceptable to the customer. They should be defined as part of the Project Brief and agreed between customer and supplier no later than the project initiation stage. They should be documented in the Project Initiation Document.

Activity network
A flow diagram showing the activities of a plan and their interdependencies. The network shows each activity's duration, earliest start and finish times, latest start and finish times and float. Also known as 'planning network'. *See also Critical path.*

Assurance
Independent assessment and confirmation that the programme as a whole or any of its aspects are on track – applying relevant practices and procedures – and that the projects, activities and business rationale remain aligned to the programme's objectives.

Baseline
A snapshot; a position or situation that is recorded. Although the position may be updated later, the baseline remains unchanged and available as a reminder of the original state and as a comparison against the current position. Products that have passed their quality checks and are approved are baselined products. Anything 'baselined' should be under version control in configuration management and 'frozen', i.e. no changes to that version are allowed.

Benefit(s)
MSP – The quantifiable and measurable improvement resulting from an outcome which is perceived as positive by a stakeholder and which will normally have a tangible value expressed in monetary or resource terms. Benefits are expected when a change is conceived. Benefits are realised as a result of activities undertaken to effect the change.

PRINCE2 – The positive outcomes, quantified or unquantified, that a project is being undertaken to deliver, and that justify the investment.

Benefit Profile (MSP)
The complete description of a benefit or dis-benefit.

Benefits management
MSP – A continuous management process running throughout the programme. It provides the programme with a target and a means of monitoring achievement against that target on a regular basis.

Benefits Management Strategy (MSP)
How the programme will handle benefits management.

Benefits realisation
PRINCE2 – The practice of ensuring that the outcome of a project produces the projected benefits claimed in the Business Case.

Blueprint (MSP)
A model of the business or organisation, its working practices and processes, the information it requires and the technology that will be needed to deliver the capability described in the Vision Statement.

Business Case (MSP and PRINCE2)
MSP – A document aggregating the specific programme information on overall costs, the anticipated benefit realisation, the timeframe, and the risk profile of the programme.

PRINCE2 – Information that describes the justification for setting up and continuing a PRINCE2 project. It provides the reasons (and answers the question 'Why?') for the project. An outline Business Case should be in the Project Mandate. Its existence is checked as part of the Project Brief, and a revised, fuller version appears in the Project Initiation Document. It is updated at key points, such as end stage assessments, throughout the project.

Business Case management
The manner in which the programme's rationale, objectives, benefits and risks are balanced against the financial investment, and this balance maintained, adjusted and assessed during the programme.

Business Change Manager (MSP)
The role responsible for benefits management, from identification through to delivery, and ensuring the implementation and embedding of the new capabilities delivered by the projects. Typically allocated to more than one individual. Alternative title: 'Change Agent'.

Capability
A service, function or operation that enables the organisation to exploit opportunities.

Change agent
See Business Change Manager.

Change authority
A group to which the Project Board may delegate responsibility for the consideration of requests for change. The change authority is given a budget and can approve changes within that budget.

Change budget
The money allocated to the change authority to be spent on authorised requests for change.

Change control
The procedure to ensure that the processing of all Project Issues is controlled, including the submission, analysis and decision-making.

Checkpoint
A team-level, time-driven review of progress, usually involving a meeting.

Checkpoint Report (PRINCE2)
A progress report of the information gathered at a checkpoint meeting, which is given by a team to the Project Manager and provides reporting data as defined in the Work Package.

Communication(s) Plan (MSP & PRINCE2)
MSP – A plan of the communications activities during the programme.

PRINCE2 – Part of the Project Initiation Document describing how the project's stakeholders and interested parties will be kept informed during the project.

Concession
An Off-Specification that is accepted by the Project Board without corrective action.

Configuration audit
A comparison of the latest version number and status of all products shown in the configuration library records against the information held by the product authors.

Configuration control
Configuration control is concerned with physically controlling receipt and issue of products, keeping track of product status, protecting finished products and controlling any changes to them.

Configuration management
A discipline, normally supported by software tools, that gives management precise control over its assets (for example, the products of a project), covering planning, identification, control, status accounting and verification of the products.

Contingency budget

The amount of money required to implement a contingency plan. If the Project Board approves a contingency plan, it would normally set aside a contingency budget, which would only be called upon if the contingency plan had to be implemented when the associated risk occurs. *See also Contingency plan.*

Contingency plan

A plan that provides details of the measures to be taken if a defined risk should occur. The plan is only implemented if the risk occurs. A contingency plan is prepared where other actions (risk prevention, reduction or transfer) are either not possible, too expensive or the current view of the risk is that the cost of the risk occurring does not sufficiently outweigh the cost of taking avoiding action – but the risk cannot be simply accepted. The Project Board can see that, should the risk occur, there is a plan of action to counter it. If the Project Board agrees that this is the best form of action, it would put aside a contingency budget, the cost of the contingency plan, again, only to be used if the risk occurs.

Critical path

This is the line connecting the start of an activity network with the final activity in that network through those activities with zero float, i.e. those activities where any delay will delay the time of the entire end date of the plan. There may be more than one such path. The sum of the activity durations on the critical path will determine the end date of the plan.

Cross-organisational programme

A programme requiring the committed involvement of more than one organisation to achieve the desired outcomes. Also referred to as 'cross-cutting programmes'.

Customer

The person or group who commissioned the work and will benefit from the end results.

Customer's quality expectations (PRINCE2)

A statement from the customer about the quality expected from the final product.

Daily Log (PRINCE2)

A record of jobs to do or to check that others have done, commitments from the author or others, important events, decisions or discussions. A Daily Log should be kept by the Project Manager and any Team Managers.

Deliverable

An item that the project has to create as part of the requirements. It may be part of the final outcome or an intermediate element on which one or more subsequent deliverables are dependent. According to the type of project, another name for a deliverable is 'product'.

Dependency network

A representation of all the inputs and outputs from the projects and how they inter-relate, treating each project as a 'black box'.

Dis-benefit
An unwanted result of an outcome; the negative quantification of an outcome.

Earned value analysis
Earned value analysis is a method for measuring project performance. It indicates how much of the budget should have been spent in view of the amount of work done so far and the task, assignment or resources.

End goal
The ultimate objective of a programme.

End Project Report (PRINCE2)
A report given by the Project Manager to the Project Board confirming the handover of all products and provides an updated Business Case and an assessment of how well the project has done against its Project Initiation Document.

End stage assessment
The review by the Project Board and Project Manager of the End Stage Report to decide whether to approve the next Stage Plan (unless the last stage has now been completed). According to the size and criticality of the project, the review may be formal or informal. The approval to proceed should be documented as an important management product.

End Stage Report (PRINCE2)
A report given by the Project Manager to the Project Board at the end of each management stage of the project. This provides information about the project performance during the stage and the project status at stage end.

Exception
A situation where it can be forecast that there will be a deviation beyond the tolerance levels agreed between Project Manager and Project Board (or between Project Board and corporate or programme management, or between a Team Manager and the Project Manager).

Exception assessment
This is a meeting of the Project Board to approve (or reject) an Exception Plan.

Exception Plan (PRINCE2)
This is a plan that often follows an Exception Report. For a Team Plan exception, it covers the period from the present to the end of the Work Package; for a Stage Plan exception, it covers the period from the present to the end of the current stage. If the exception were at a project level, the Project Plan would be replaced.

Exception Report (PRINCE2)
Description of the exception situation, its impact, options, recommendation and impact of the recommendation to the Project Board. This report is prepared by the relevant manager to inform the next higher level of management of the situation.

Executive (PRINCE2)

The single individual with overall responsibility for ensuring that a project meets its objectives and delivers the projected benefits. This individual should ensure that the project or programme maintains its business focus, that it has clear authority and that the work, including risks, is actively managed. The Executive is the chairperson of the Project Board, representing the customer, and is the owner of the Business Case.

Feasibility study

A feasibility study is an early study of a problem to assess if a solution is feasible. The study will normally scope the problem, identify and explore a number of solutions and make a recommendation on what action to take. Part of the work in developing options is to calculate an outline Business Case for each as one aspect of comparison.

Follow-on Action Recommendations (PRINCE2)

A report that can be used as input to the process of creating a Business Case/Project Mandate for any follow-on PRINCE2 project and for recording any follow-on instructions covering incomplete products or outstanding Project Issues.

Gantt chart

This is a diagram of a plan's activities against a time background, showing start and end times and resources required.

Gate/Gateway review

MSP – A formal and independent review of the programme (or project) providing assurance on whether the programme is operating effectively and is likely to achieve its outcomes.

PRINCE2 – A generic term, rather than a PRINCE2 term, meaning a point at the end of a stage or phase where a decision is made whether to continue with the project. In PRINCE2 this would equate to an end stage assessment.

Governance

The functions, responsibilities, processes and procedures that define how the programme is set up, managed and controlled.

Highlight Report (PRINCE2)

Report from the Project Manager to the Project Board on a time-driven frequency on stage progress.

Issue

MSP – A problem, query, concern or change request that affects the programme and requires management intervention and action to resolve.

PRINCE2 – A term used to cover any concern, query, Request for Change, suggestion or Off-Specification raised during the project. They can be about anything to do with the project. *See also Project Issue*.

Issue Log (MSP and PRINCE2)

MSP – The log of all issues raised during the programme.

PRINCE2 – Contains all Project Issues including Requests for Change raised during the project. Project Issues are each allocated a unique number and are filed in the Issue Log under the appropriate status. *See also Project Issue.*

Issue Resolution Strategy (MSP)

How the programme will handle issue resolution.

Lessons Learned Log (PRINCE2)

An informal collection of good and bad lessons learned about the management and specialist processes and products as the project progresses. At the end of the project, it is formalised and structured into a Lessons Learned Report. *See also Lessons Learned Report.*

Lessons Learned Report (PRINCE2)

A report that describes the lessons learned in undertaking the project and that includes statistics from the quality control of the project's management products. It is approved by the Project Board and then held centrally for the benefit of future projects.

Off-Specification (PRINCE2)

Something that should be provided by the project, but currently is not (or is forecast not to be) provided. This might be a missing product or a product not meeting its specifications. It is one type of Project Issue.

Operational and maintenance acceptance

Acceptance by the person/group who will support the product during its useful life, that it is accepted into the operational environment. The format of the acceptance will depend on the product itself. It could be in the form of an acceptance letter signed by the appropriate authority, or a more complex report detailing the operational and maintenance arrangements that have been put in place.

Outcome

MSP – The result of change, normally affecting real-world behaviour and/or circumstances. Outcomes are desired when a change is conceived. Outcomes are achieved as a result of the activities undertaken to effect the change.

PRINCE2 – The term used to describe the totality of what the project is set up to deliver, consisting of all the specialist products. For example, this could be an installed computer system with trained staff to use it, backed up by new working practices and documentation, a refurbished and equipped building with all the staff moved in and working, or it could be a new product launched with a recruited and trained sales and support team in place.

Peer review

Peer reviews are specific reviews of a project or any of its products where personnel from within the organisation and/or from other organisations carry out an independent assessment of the project. Peer reviews can be done at any point within a project but are often used at stage-end points.

Phase

A part, section or segment of a project, similar in meaning to a PRINCE2 stage. The key meaning of stage in PRINCE2 terms is the use of management stages, i.e. sections of the project to which the Project Board only commits one at a time. A phase might be more connected to a time slice, change of skills required or change of emphasis.

Portfolio management

The co-ordination of a number of projects.

Post-implementation review

See post-project review.

Post-project review

One or more reviews held after project closure to determine if the expected benefits have been obtained. Also known as 'post-implementation review'.

PRINCE2

A method that supports some selected aspects of project management. The acronym stands for **PR**ojects **IN C**ontrolled **E**nvironments.

PRINCE2 project

A project whose product(s) can be defined at its start sufficiently precisely so as to be measurable against predefined metrics, and that is managed according to the PRINCE2 method.

Process

That which must be done to bring about a particular result, in terms of information to be gathered, decisions to be made and results that must be achieved.

Producer

This role represents the creator(s) of a product that is the subject of a quality review. Typically, it will be filled by the person who has produced the product or who has led the team responsible.

Product

MSP – Any input or output that can be identified and described in a tangible, measurable way.

PRINCE2 – Any input to or output from a project. PRINCE2 distinguishes between management products (which are produced as part of the management or quality processes of the project) and specialist products (which are those products that make up the final deliverable). A product may itself be a collection of other products.

Product-based planning

A four-step technique leading to a comprehensive plan based on creation and delivery of required outputs. The technique considers prerequisite products, quality requirements and the dependencies between products.

Product Breakdown Structure (PRINCE2)

A hierarchy of all the products to be produced during a plan.

Product Checklist (PRINCE2)

A list of the major products of a plan, plus key dates in their delivery.

Product Description (PRINCE2)

A description of a product's purpose, composition, derivation and quality criteria. It is produced at planning time, as soon as possible after the need for the product is identified.

Product Flow Diagram (PRINCE2)

A diagram showing the sequence of production and interdependencies of the products listed in a Product Breakdown Structure.

Product Life Span

This is the term used in the PRINCE2 manual to define the total life of the product from the time of the initial idea for the product until it is removed from service. It is likely that there will be many projects affecting the product during its life, such as feasibility study, development and enhancement or correction.

Product Status Account (PRINCE2)

A report on the status of products. The required products can be specified by identifier or the part of the project in which they were developed.

Programme

MSP – A portfolio of projects and activities that are co-ordinated and managed as a unit such that they achieve outcomes and realise benefits.

PRINCE2 – A portfolio of projects selected, planned and managed in a co-ordinated way.

Programme Board (MSP)

A group or committee that may be established to assist with the direction-setting and leadership of a programme. The Sponsoring Group may form a Programme Board.

Programme Brief (MSP)

An outline description of the programme's objectives, desired benefits, risks, costs and timeframe.

Programme Definition (MSP)

The collection of information defining the programme covering: Vision Statement, Blueprint, Business Case, organisation structure, Project Portfolio, Benefit Profiles, Stakeholder Map.

Programme Director (MSP)

The title previously used for the role with ultimate accountability for the programme – 'Senior Responsible Owner' is the title used in the MSP guide.

Programme management

The co-ordinated organisation, direction and implementation of a portfolio of projects and activities that together achieve outcomes and realise benefits that are of strategic importance.

Programme Manager (MSP)

The role responsible for the set-up, management and delivery of the programme. Typically allocated to a single individual.

Programme Mandate (MSP)

The trigger for the programme from senior management who are sponsoring the programme.

Programme Office (MSP)

The function providing the information hub for the programme and its delivery objectives.

Programme organisation

How the programme will be managed throughout its lifecycle, the roles and responsibilities of individuals involved in the programme, and personnel management or human resources arrangements.

Programme Plan (MSP)

A comprehensive document scheduling the projects, their costs, resources, risks, and transition activities together with monitoring and control activities.

Project

MSP – A particular way of managing activities to deliver specific outputs over a specified period and within cost, quality and resource constraints.

PRINCE2 – A temporary organisation that is created for the purpose of delivering one or more business products according to a specified Business Case.

Project Approach (PRINCE2)

A description of the way in which the work of the project is to be approached. For example: Are we building a product from scratch or buying in a product that already exists? Are the technology and products that we can use constrained by decisions taken at programme level?

Project Assurance (PRINCE2)

The Project Board's responsibilities to assure itself that the project is being conducted correctly.

Project Brief (PRINCE2)

A description of what the project is to do; a refined and extended version of the Project Mandate, which the Project Board approves, and which is input to project initiation.

Project closure notification
Advice from the Project Board to inform all stakeholders and the host location that the project resources can be disbanded and support services, such as space, equipment and access, demobilised. It should indicate a closure date for costs to be charged to the project.

Project closure recommendation
A recommendation prepared by the Project Manager for the Project Board to send as a project closure notification when the board is satisfied that the project can be closed.

Project Initiation Document (PID) (PRINCE2)
A logical document that brings together the key information needed to start the project on a sound basis and to convey that information to all concerned with the project.

Project Issue (PRINCE2)
A term used to cover any concern, query, Request for Change, suggestion or Off-Specification raised during the project. They can be about anything to do with the project.

Project Life Cycle
This term is used in this manual to define the period from the start-up of a project to the handover of the finished product to those who will operate and maintain it.

Project management
The planning, monitoring and control of all aspects of the project and the motivation of all those involved in it to achieve the project objectives on time and to the specified cost, quality and performance.

Project management team
Covers the entire management structure of Project Board, Project Manager, plus any Team Manager, Project Assurance and Project Support roles.

Project Manager (PRINCE2)
The person given the authority and responsibility to manage the project on a day-to-day basis to deliver the required products within the constraints agreed with the Project Board.

Project Mandate (PRINCE2)
Information created externally to the project, which forms the terms of reference and is used to start up the PRINCE2 project.

Project Plan (PRINCE2)
A high-level plan showing the major products of the project, when they will be delivered and at what cost. An initial Project Plan is presented as part of the Project Initiation Document. This is revised as information on actual progress appears. It is a major control document for the Project Board to measure actual progress against expectations.

Project Portfolio (MSP)
A list of all the projects and activities that together will deliver the required 'future state'

described in the Blueprint and hence achieve the capabilities expressed in the Vision Statement.

Project Quality Plan (PRINCE2)

A plan defining the key quality criteria, quality control and audit processes to be applied to project management and specialist work in the PRINCE2 project. It will be part of the text in the Project Initiation Document.

Project records

A collection of all approved management and specialist products and other material, which is necessary to provide an auditable record of the project (NB: this does not include working files).

Project start-up notification

Advice to the host location that the project is about to start and requesting any required Project Support services.

Project Support (PRINCE2)

Project Support is an administrative role in the project management team. Project Support can be in the form of advice and help with project management tools, guidance, administrative services such as filing, and the collection of actual data. The provision of any Project Support on a formal basis is optional. Tasks need to be done by the Project Manager or delegated to a separate body and this will be driven by the needs of the individual project and Project Manager.

One support function that must be considered is that of Configuration Management. Depending on the project size and environment, there may be a need to formalise this and it quickly becomes a task with which the Project Manager cannot cope without support.

Project Support Office (PRINCE2)

A group set up to provide certain administrative services to the Project Manager. Often the group provides its services to many projects in parallel.

Proximity (of risk)

Reflects the timing of the risk, i.e.: Is the threat (or opportunity) stronger at a particular time, or does it disappear sometime in the future? Or does the probability or impact change over time?

Quality

The totality of features and characteristics of a product or service that bear on its ability to satisfy stated needs. Also defined as 'fitness for purpose' or 'conforms to requirements'.

Quality Log (PRINCE2)

Contains all planned and completed quality activities. The Quality Log is used by the Project Manager and Project Assurance as part of reviewing progress.

Quality Management Strategy (MSP)
How the programme will achieve the required levels of quality in the way the programme is managed and directed, and how the programme's deliverables will be assessed for 'fitness for purpose'.

Quality Management System
The complete set of quality standards, procedures and responsibilities for a site or organisation.

Quality review
A quality review is a quality checking technique with a specific structure, defined roles and procedure designed to ensure a product's completeness and adherence to standards. The participants are drawn from those with an interest in the product and those with the necessary skills to review its correctness. An example of the checks made by a quality review is, 'Does the document match the quality criteria in the Product Description?'.

Quality system
See Quality Management System.

Requirements
A description of the user's needs. *See also Specification.*

Request for Change (PRINCE2)
A means of proposing a modification to the current specification of a product. It is one type of Project Issue.

Resource Management Strategy (MSP)
Description of the resource requirements for the programme and how they will be managed.

Reviewer
A person asked to review a product that is the subject of a quality review.

Risk
MSP – A negative threat (or potential positive opportunity) that might affect the course of the programme.

PRINCE2 – Risk can be defined as uncertainty of outcome, whether positive opportunity or negative threat. Every project has risks associated with it. Project management has the task of identifying risks that apply and taking appropriate steps to take advantage of opportunities that may arise and avoid, reduce or react to threats.

Risk Log (MSP and PRINCE2)
MSP – The log of all risks identified during the programme. Often called the 'Risk Register'.

PRINCE2 – Contains all information about the risks, their analysis, countermeasures and status. Also known as Risk Register.

Risk Management Strategy (MSP)

How the programme will establish and maintain an effective risk management regime on the programme.

Risk profile

A graphical representation of information normally found on the Risk Log.

Risk Register (MSP)

See Risk Log.

Risk tolerance line

The risk tolerance line is one drawn between risks that can be accepted or for which suitable actions have been planned, and risks that are considered sufficiently serious to require referral to the next higher level of project authority.

Role

A particular set of responsibilities and accountabilities that may be allocated to one or more individuals. In some circumstances, roles may be merged together as long as there is no conflict of interest.

Senior Responsible Owner (MSP)

MSP – The title given to the individual who is ultimately accountable for successful delivery, that is, the successful achievement of desired outcomes and realisation of expected benefits from a programme. This role was previously referred to as 'Programme Director'.

PRINCE2 – This is not a PRINCE2 term, but is used in many organisations. Its equivalent in PRINCE2 terms would be the 'Executive' role. *See also Executive.*

Senior Supplier (PRINCE2)

The Project Board role that provides knowledge and experience of the main discipline(s) involved in the production of the project's deliverable(s). Represents the supplier(s) interests within the project and provides supplier resources.

Senior User (PRINCE2)

A Project Board role, accountable for ensuring that user needs are specified correctly and that the solution meets those needs.

Specification

A detailed statement of what the user wants in terms of products, what these should look like, what they should do and with what they should interface.

Sponsor

Not a specific PRINCE2 role but often used to mean the major driving force of a project. May be the equivalent of Executive or corporate/programme management.

Sponsoring Group (MSP)
Senior-level sponsorship of the programme providing the investment decision and top-level endorsement of the rationale and objectives for the programme. May be known as 'Programme Board'.

Stakeholder(s)
MSP – An individual, group or organisation with an interest in, or influence over, the programme.

PRINCE2 – Parties with an interest in the execution and outcome of a project. They would include business streams affected by or dependent on the outcome of a project.

Stakeholder Management Strategy (MSP)
How the programme will identify and analyse the stakeholders and how ongoing communications will be achieved between the programme and all its stakeholders.

Stakeholder Map (MSP)
A matrix showing stakeholders and their particular interests in the programme.

Stage
A stage is the section of the project that the Project Manager is managing on behalf of the Project Board at any one time, at the end of which the Project Board wishes to review progress to date, the state of the Project Plan, Business Case and risks, and the next Stage Plan in order to decide whether to continue with the project.

Supplier
The group or groups responsible for the supply of the project's specialist products.

Team Manager (PRINCE2)
A role that may be employed by the Project Manager or Senior Supplier to manage the work of project team members.

Tolerance
The permissible deviation above and below a plan's estimate of time and cost without escalating the deviation to the next level of management. Separate tolerance figures should be given for time and cost. There may also be tolerance levels for quality, scope, benefit and risk. Tolerance is applied at project, stage and team levels.

Tranche
A group of projects structured around distinct step changes in capability and benefit delivery.

User(s)
The person or group who will use the final deliverable(s) of the project.

Value management

A management technique to define the perceived and actual value to the organisation, and then assessing progress and achievements based on this value.

Vision Statement (MSP)

An outward-facing description of the new capabilities resulting from programme delivery.

Work Package (PRINCE2)

The set of information relevant to the creation of one or more products. It will contain a description of the work, the Product Description(s), details of any constraints on production such as time and cost, interfaces and confirmation of the agreement between the Project Manager and the person or Team Manager who is to implement the Work Package that the work can be done within the constraints.

FURTHER READING

- *Managing Successful Programmes (MSP)*. ISBN 0 11 330917 1. Published by The Stationery Office, www.tsoshop.co.uk

- *Managing Successful Projects with PRINCE2 (PRINCE2)*. ISBN 0 11 330946 5. Published by The Stationery Office, www.tsoshop.co.uk

- *Management of Risk: Guidance for Practitioners (M_o_R)*. ISBN 0 11 330909 0. Published by The Stationery Office, www.tsoshop.co.uk

- *How to Manage Business Change*. ISBN 1 90 309110 1. Published by Format Publishing.

- *Successful IT: Modernising Government in Action (McCartney Report)*. ISBN 0 11 702533 X. Published by The Stationery Office, www.tsoshop.co.uk

- Common Causes of Project Failure. Available at http://www.ogc.gov.uk/sdtoolkit/reference/ogc_library/bestpracticebriefings/causesprojfailure.pdf

- OGC Maturity Models in the Capability and Capacity section of the SDTK. Available at http://www.ogc.gov.uk/sdtoolkit/reference/tools/

INDEX

Note: The index does not contain references to the glossary. Diagrams and windows on practice are shown in **bold** type